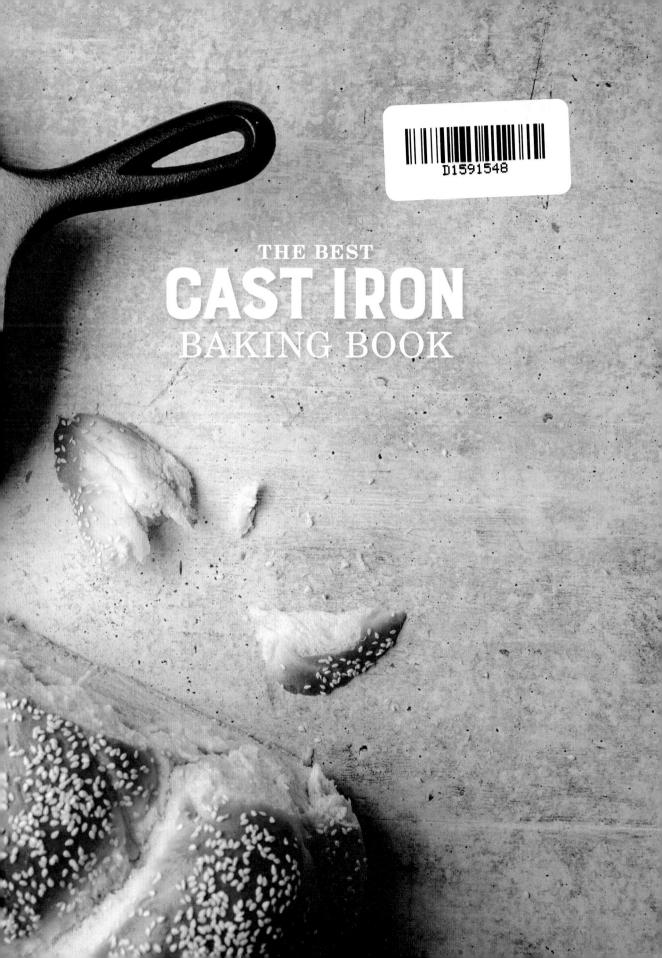

THE BEST
CAST IRON
BAKING BOOK

THE BEST
CAST IRON
BAKING BOOK

Recipes for Breads, Pies, Biscuits & More

ROXANNE WYSS & KATHY MOORE

Robert
ROSE

For complete cataloging information, see page 192.

Disclaimer
The recipes in this book have been carefully tested by our kitchen and our
tasters. To the best of our knowledge, they are safe and nutritious for ordinary
use and users. For those people with food or other allergies, or who have
special food requirements or health issues, please read the suggested contents
of each recipe carefully and determine whether or not they may create a
problem for you. All recipes are used at the risk of the consumer.

   We cannot be responsible for any hazards, loss or damage that may occur
as a result of any recipe use.

   For those with special needs, allergies, requirements or health problems, in
the event of any doubt, please contact your medical adviser prior to the use of
any recipe.

At the time of publication, all URLs referenced link to existing websites. Robert
Rose Inc. is not responsible for maintaining, and does not endorse the content
of, any website or content not created by Robert Rose Inc.

COVER & BOOK DESIGN: Kevin Cockburn/PageWave Graphics Inc.

COVER & INTERIOR PHOTOGRAPHY: Brian Samuels

FOOD & PROP STYLING: Brian Samuels & Rebecca Arnold Saenz

EDITOR: Meredith Dees

COPYEDITOR & INDEXER: Gillian Watts

PROOFREADER: Kelly Jones

Published by Robert Rose Inc.
120 Eglinton Avenue East, Suite 800, Toronto, Ontario, Canada M4P 1E2
Tel: (416) 322-6552 Fax: (416) 322-6936
www.robertrose.ca

Printed and bound in Canada

1 2 3 4 5 6 7 8 9 MI 29 28 27 26 25 24 23 22 21

*We dedicate this book to our moms
and grandmas, who paved a culinary
path for us by cherishing and using
their cast-iron cookware, and to
cooks we hope to inspire. We would
be remiss if we did not also dedicate
this book to the families who managed
to work, cook and teach their way
through the pandemic — we hope for
a more positive future.*

CONTENTS

THE THRILL AND PASSION OF COOKING WITH CAST IRON

A cast-iron skillet is as enticing as the sizzle you hear when the bacon crisps or when the butter dances in the pan. It is as alluring as the aroma of the bread baking in the oven or as tempting as a warm chocolate chip skillet cookie nestled under cold ice cream.

That same cast-iron pan is as precious as your splattered note card for Grandma's biscuits, the one she wrote out for you many years ago. It is as memorable as the cinnamon rolls your family always serves for the holidays. It is simmering with the stories of family meals and campfire stews. Cast iron is exalted in love letters, praised in poems and bequeathed in wills.

Perhaps no other pan or utensil cooks up as many memories and as much up-to-the-minute goodness as black cast-iron cookware.

Like many, we each inherited cast-iron cookware from our mothers and grandmothers. We cherish those skillets, and every time we use them, we are connected to our loving families, whose cooking inspires us even today. We feel their presence and know that, each time we pick up that skillet or Dutch oven, we are touching the hands of our ancestors who fried chicken and baked biscuits in that same cookware.

When you buy new cast iron, you can trust that generations to come will cook in that same pan and feel your devotion and passion. Cooking in cast iron simultaneously connects you with your past and your future.

Whether on the stovetop or in the oven, cast-iron cooking is unsurpassed. Yet many in our cooking classes are surprised when we describe cast-iron baking. We promise you, it is wonderful and easy! These breads, biscuits, cobblers, pies, cakes, pizzas and brownies embody both up-to-date deliciousness and traditional lusciousness. Unbeatable old-fashioned flavors take on new ease and fresh tastes in these thoroughly tested recipes.

So many people, from top chefs to your neighbor next door, know the wonders of cast iron and shout passionately about using it. Just browse the copious number of Facebook groups or scan the hashtags on social media to see its popularity. Now, with *The Best Cast Iron Baking Book*, everyone can enjoy using their cast iron confidently. If you have been wanting to make cast iron your go-to skillet, this cookbook will be your guide.

We are thrilled to invite you into a whole new world of baking. Now pick up that trusty black skillet or Dutch oven and get into the kitchen!

— *Roxanne & Kathy*

CAST-IRON CONFIDENCE

The Benefits of Cast-Iron Cookware

VERSATILE Cast iron is ideal for cooking nearly any food. This one pan can go from a burner on the stove into the oven, or even outside to the grill. Many a camper and Scout remember cooking stews and cobblers in cast iron on the bonfire. It is the one piece of cookware that great cooks turn to for frying, braising, roasting, simmering, baking, stewing, sautéing and broiling. Perhaps your favorite restaurant even uses a cast-iron skillet as a chic serving piece. Plus, if your kitchen is small or you wish to downsize, a few wisely chosen pieces of cast iron can cook it all.

DURABLE Sturdy, nearly indestructible cast-iron cookware will last for a lifetime, and probably for generations. It will not scratch like a new shiny pot or nonstick coated skillet. You can grab a metal spatula or spoon and not worry about marring the surface. And, if it does rust or you come across a discarded cast-iron piece at a flea market, you can restore it to just as good as, if not better than, new. (See page 14 for more information about seasoning and restoring cookware.)

REACHES HIGH HEAT This cookware withstands the high temperatures needed for searing a steak, caramelizing fruit and deep-frying. Standard instructions for most nonstick coated cookware recommend using only low to medium heat, so if you want to use a higher temperature, cast iron is the best choice.

RETAINS HEAT Once the cast iron is hot, you will not have hot spots or notice heat fluctuations the way you would when cooking in a thin metal pan that reacts to normal heat cycles on the stove. When baking, that same heat distribution will mean that the crust browns evenly. You can capture and use that residual heat for serving, too. A casserole, a cobbler, a dip or those biscuits will stay warm for serving.

IMPROVES WITH AGE Like fine wines and elegant antiques, cast iron improves with age. Most pans lose their shine, scratch, stain or chip, but every time you use cast-iron cookware, the surface becomes shinier, more nonstick and well-seasoned.

NONSTICK The slick surface of seasoned cast iron means you can cook lots of different foods with little or no added oil or fat. Whether it is a cheesy casserole or a sweet and gooey dessert, that cast-iron skillet cleans up in a snap.

HEALTH The natural nonstick surface of well-used cast iron is desired by many, as there are no chemical coatings applied, so there is no need to worry about chips of coating flaking off into your food. (You may have heard that cooking in cast iron will provide beneficial iron, a nutrient needed in your diet, but current studies do not support this myth.)

FLAVOR That golden brown chewy crust on a cookie or bread, the sear on a steak that locks in the juiciness, and hot and crisp pizza and pie crusts mean unbeatable flavor.

Top Tips

- Use it often. Dry it well. That is really all you need to know to use and preserve your cast iron.

- The more you cook in cast iron, the better it becomes and the faster the surface takes on a shine so foods don't stick. This is what we call a well-seasoned piece.

- Use heavy-duty oven mitts! Remember, cast-iron handles get hot and stay hot. Plus, those handles look the same whether hot or cold, and they will stay hot for quite some time.

- Cast iron performs perfectly on the stove. However, when cooking with cast iron on a burner, always start on low heat. It can move readily from the burner to the oven and back to the burner, or you can even use it out on the grill or over a fire. (We keep a separate cast-iron piece for use on the grill, as the exterior of the pan can build up black residue from the fire.)

- Always put hot cast iron on a wire rack or heatproof surface. Never put a hot cast-iron skillet on a finished table, laminate countertop or even a granite or quartz surface. It will mar the surface, leave burn marks or scars and, in extreme situations, could crack your countertop.

- If you have a smooth glass cooktop, be extra cautious not to slide the cast iron and scratch the surface, or, worse, drop it and crack the cooktop.

- Yes, you can use metal spoons and spatulas with cast iron. Even sharp kitchen tools and knives won't hurt the surface. However, a rubber scraper that is not heatproof can melt.

- Review and follow the manufacturer's recommendations for your new cast-iron cookware and for the stove or oven you are using.

- Cast iron can safely go into a preheated oven. For some recipes, it may be placed in a cold oven and heated along with the oven.

- Cast iron holds heat. When baking, take the pan out of the oven a minute or two before the food is fully baked and let the residual heat finish the baking. If you leave it in the oven until the food tests done, it might overcook a little before the cast iron cools.

- Want a crispy crust? Preheat the cast iron, then add the batter or dough. For a more tender crust, put the batter or dough in a cold pan.

REGULAR VS. ENAMELED CAST IRON

Some may call those classic black cast-iron pieces "regular" or "uncoated" cast iron. This is the type of pan we used for the recipes in this book. Enameled cast iron has been coated in a porcelain enamel, so it is shiny and is available in a variety of colors. These pieces are more expensive than regular cast iron, will not rust and do not require seasoning, but they can chip.

Maintenance

Cleaning your cast iron is easy: Simply wash it in hot water and, if need be, use a nylon brush. (However, if you are using an enameled cast-iron pan, refer to the manufacturer's instructions.) Yes, you can wash it in soapy water, and we do, especially after cooking fish or something really sticky. Just don't soak it in soapy water, and never place it in the dishwasher.

One word of caution: If the cast iron is hot, let it cool slightly before washing. Thermal shock — the sudden change from hot to cold — can cause cast iron to crack. If the piece is hot, do not submerge it in cold water or pour cold water into it.

Make sure to dry cast iron thoroughly. We dry it with a paper towel and then, just to be sure, we often put it back in the warm oven or on a burner over low heat to be sure it is absolutely dry.

To maintain your pan, wipe the warm cast iron with a light coat of vegetable oil — about $\frac{1}{2}$ tsp (2 mL) — to ensure it stays dry and prevents moisture contact. Do not use too much oil or let it pool in the cookware, as the surface could become sticky or the oil rancid.

If the pan is stored damp, it will rust. While rust sounds terrible, all is not lost. You can wash it, then season it (see below) and get back to cooking — but better safe than sorry.

Seasoning

What does "seasoning" cast iron mean? No, we don't mean the salt, pepper and spices sprinkled on food. For cast-iron cookware, seasoning creates a natural nonstick surface. While it may sound a bit daunting, seasoning is what happens to the skillet or Dutch oven every time you use it. That is why we tell you to cook in it often.

In the simplest of terms, seasoning means the fat molecules become linked together and almost bonded to the surface of the iron. While you do not need to know all the scientific terms (like polymerization), the short of it is that the iron takes on a natural nonstick patina. Just use it and watch it become slick, shiny, well-seasoned and the best nonstick pan you've ever used.

If you dry your cast iron, rub it lightly with oil and then store it. You will probably not need to season it again. If you purchase a new piece of cast iron today, the label will probably tell you it is "pre-seasoned," so you can jump over the next few paragraphs. However, if you find that your cast iron was put away damp or if you uncover an old piece, it is easy to reclaim it and restore the seasoning.

STEPS TO SEASONING CAST IRON

First, how do you know if you need to season your cast iron? If you find foods often stick, go ahead and season it. If it has a dull, splotchy finish, it needs to be seasoned. If that cast-iron piece has been stored for some time or is one you inherited, it probably needs to be seasoned. Follow the steps below:

1 Wash the pan in hot water. If need be, wash it quickly in hot, soapy water with a nylon brush. Do not soak it. Dry it thoroughly.

2 Rub the entire surface of the skillet or pot — inside, outside, handles and lid — with about 1 tbsp (15 mL) vegetable oil. Do not use olive oil, butter, bacon grease or lard. Unsaturated oils like vegetable oil

and canola oil work best. (You could use flaxseed or grapeseed oil, but that's not necessary, and they haven't been proven better than less expensive vegetable oils.) While a little oil is great, do not think that more is the way to go. Excess oil will pool and the finish will become sticky instead of smooth and shiny.

3 Place the oiled cast iron upside down on the middle rack of your oven. If it has a lid, put it on the same rack, nestled beside the skillet or pot. Place a baking sheet or aluminum foil on the rack underneath to catch any drips that might occur.

4 Turn the oven to 350°F (180°C). (Do not preheat the oven first.) Bake the pieces for 1 hour. Turn off the oven and let the cast-iron pieces cool completely before removing them. The cast iron should now have a sheen and be ready to go.

5 If the cast iron is in bad condition and this process doesn't create the sheen you want, repeat the seasoning steps.

EXTREME CLEANING 101

Extreme Rust? Try soaking your cast iron in vinegar water before washing and seasoning. Combine about 2 cups (500 mL) white vinegar and 1 gallon (4 L) water. Soak the cast iron for about 1 hour, then scrub it. If the rust is gone, season the pan and you have reclaimed your cast iron. If rust is still present, repeat the soaking once or twice, then season again.

Off Smell? Bake the dry, empty cast iron to remove odors. Put the piece in a cold oven. Heat the oven to 400°F (200°C) and bake the cast iron for 15 minutes.

Sticky Surface? If the surface has become sticky, put the dry, empty piece in a cold oven. Heat the oven to 450°F (230°C) and bake the cast iron for 1 hour. Then reseason.

Food Residue or Residual Odor? Scrubbing your cast iron with a paste of salt and water is a quick way to remove a little food residue or residual odor.

BAKING 101

Equipment

WHAT CAST IRON DO YOU NEED FOR THIS BOOK?

This cookbook uses two kitchen workhorses: a 10-inch (25 cm) skillet and a round 5-quart (4.7 L) Dutch oven with a lid. If you do not know what size skillet or Dutch oven you have, here is how to measure them:

SKILLET A skillet is measured across the inside at the top edge. If your skillet is about 10 to $10\frac{1}{4}$ inches (25 to 26 cm), it is ideal for these recipes. If you are using a larger or smaller skillet than the one specified in the recipe, the recipe will have to be adapted and the baking time adjusted. Generally, fill the skillet about one-half to two-thirds full; do not overfill or underfill it. Check the cooking progress and bake until the food is done, but do not overbake.

DUTCH OVEN A Dutch oven is measured to overflow capacity. We have specified a 5-quart (4.7 L) covered pot for these recipes. Fill your pot with water, measuring the water in a liquid measuring cup, and note the volume just as it begins to overflow.

OTHER HELPFUL OR NECESSARY EQUIPMENT

- Bench scraper
- Bowls
- Electric stand mixer or handheld mixer
- Heatproof spatula
- Instant-read thermometer
- Liquid and dry measuring cups and spoons
- Offset spatula
- Parchment paper (see box, page 18)
- Pastry blender
- Pastry brush
- Rolling pin
- Sharp knives
- Tester
- Wire cooling rack
- Whisk

PARCHMENT PAPER 101

We are a fan of parchment paper, a grease- and moisture-proof paper frequently used for baking. We use it to line the bottom of baking pans, including cast iron.

Use a 15-inch (30 cm) square of parchment paper to line the cast-iron skillet or Dutch oven. When lining the skillet, the corners of the paper will extend upward a little. Do not let the paper extend so far that it touches the heating element or the side walls of the oven.

When baking no-knead bread, we recommend using parchment paper. Transfer the sticky dough onto a piece of lightly floured parchment. When the Dutch oven is hot, lift the corners of the paper, with the dough in the center, and carefully place it in the pan. (Use caution, as the Dutch oven will be very hot.) The weight of the dough will position the parchment paper down in the Dutch oven. Cover it with the lid. The edges of the paper will extend up toward the top. To remove the hot bread, use a heatproof spatula.

Remember, parchment paper will burn. It should never contact the heating element in the oven, or you will risk a fire.

The Pantry

Baking most breads and desserts begins with a few basic ingredients, such as flour, sugar, butter, eggs and yeast. With a well-stocked pantry, you can decide at a moment's notice to bake for your family and create wonderful, delicious foods. Here are our tips and suggestions for ingredients we use most in this book.

BUTTER Unsalted stick butter was used for the recipes in this cookbook. For optimum flavor, we do not recommend margarine. Low-fat, light, soft, diet, whipped or tub-style butters all have a different formulation than stick butter and are not recommended for these recipes. We like to buy butter when it goes on sale and keep it frozen (it can stay frozen for up to 6 months). You can also purchase good brands of butter, often at a discount, at warehouse and discount stores.

SOFTENING BUTTER

When butter is softened, that means a slight indention remains when it is touched lightly, but the butter still holds its shape. To soften butter, remove it from the refrigerator about 30 to 60 minutes before baking (depending on the temperature of the kitchen), but do not let it sit out for several hours on a hot afternoon. To soften it quickly, you can grate cold butter with a box grater. Or you can cut the butter into pieces and place it on a microwave-safe plate. Microwave on Medium-Low for 10 to 15 seconds for ¼ cup (60 mL) butter, or about 20 to 25 seconds for ½ cup (125 mL) butter, then let it stand for 10 minutes. Do not melt the butter unless the recipe calls for melted butter.

CHOCOLATE The array of baking chocolates has exploded, with many varieties, origins and artisan products now available. While all of them taste good, the choice can be confusing. Common baking chocolates include unsweetened, semisweet and bittersweet, and chips are now available in semisweet, dark, milk, white and even flavors like mint.

Dark chocolate, which we typically think of as bittersweet, is frequently labeled with the percentage of cacao in the bar, often from approximately 50 to 80 percent and occasionally up to 100 percent. Generally, the higher the percentage of cacao, the less sweet the taste. Every variety has a slightly different level of sweetness and overall flavor, but we find that in our recipes you can usually substitute one variety of baking chocolate for another.

Candy bars, on the other hand, often have sugar as their primary ingredient. We do not recommend substituting a candy bar for baking chocolate.

CREAM AND SOUR CREAM Dairy products such as sour cream, half-and-half (10%) cream and heavy or whipping (35%) cream are common ingredients in baked goods. If you substitute low-fat or fat-free items for the standard full-fat variety, the flavor and the texture will be affected. Be sure to note the "sell-by" date before you purchase dairy products, so you buy the freshest ones available — sometimes they are hiding in the back of the dairy case.

EGGS Large eggs were used for testing these recipes. Results will not be consistent if you use medium or extra-large eggs, or an egg substitute.

FLOUR The type of flour to use is indicated for each recipe. Always use the type specified, since substituting a whole wheat flour for all-purpose, for example, will affect the results. We often use unbleached all-purpose flour because it is so commonly available. Flour does not need to be sifted for the recipes in this book.

For yeast breads, you may use bread flour if you wish. Bread flour has a higher protein content, which gives strength to the dough and allows it to rise more. When making yeast breads, you can substitute the same amount of bread flour for all-purpose flour. Do not use bread flour for biscuits, pie crusts, brownies, cakes or other baking.

Watch out for sales, especially before holidays, and you can stock up on flour. It can be stored in tightly sealed containers for up to about 6 months in a cool, dry place. Store whole wheat and whole-grain flours, tightly sealed, in the freezer.

MILK AND BUTTERMILK The standard for cooking is whole milk, but we realize that many people today choose low-fat milk. Whole milk will provide the best flavor and texture, but lower-fat milk will also work. These recipes were tested using fresh dairy milk.

We love the flavor of buttermilk for its delicious tang, but far more importantly, its acidic nature affects the leavening, so do not substitute whole or nondairy milk for buttermilk.

We use buttermilk frequently and want to keep it on hand, so we freeze it in an ice-cube tray. Once frozen, pop out the buttermilk cubes and seal them in a resealable freezer bag to store. Thaw the amount you need in the refrigerator in a covered small bowl or jar, or heat in the microwave on Low (10% power) in 10-second intervals or until thawed. The buttermilk will separate, so whisk or shake it to combine before using. For optimum flavor, use frozen buttermilk within about 3 months.

DON'T HAVE BUTTERMILK?

Do not despair if you don't have any buttermilk. Pour 1 tbsp (15 mL) white vinegar or freshly squeezed lemon juice into a liquid measuring cup and add milk to equal 1 cup (250 mL). Let stand for 5 minutes, then measure out the volume you need for the recipe you are preparing. Need less buttermilk? Mix the amount you need, using the same ratio. For example, for ½ cup (125 mL), begin with 1½ tsp (7 mL) freshly squeezed lemon juice or white vinegar and add milk to equal ½ cup (125 mL). For ⅓ cup (75 mL), begin with 1 tsp (5 mL) lemon juice or white vinegar and add milk to equal ⅓ cup (75 mL).

NUTS Nuts add flavor and texture to baking. We use pecans, walnuts and almonds most frequently in this book. Toasting intensifies their flavor, so most of our recipes call for toasted nuts.

TOASTING NUTS

To toast nuts, spread them in a single layer on a rimmed baking sheet. Bake at 350°F (180°C) for 5 to 7 minutes or until lightly toasted.

OIL For baking we typically turn to canola or vegetable oil, which are flavorless ("neutral") oils. Occasionally for a specialty bread such as focaccia, we use olive oil for its flavor. There is no need to use extra-virgin olive oil for baking. Keep the extra-virgin olive oil for salad dressings, where the delicious fresh flavor will be more obvious.

NONSTICK COOKING SPRAY

Do not spray your cast-iron cookware with nonstick cooking spray. Commercial nonstick sprays contain added chemicals and emulsifiers that can build up and harm cast iron. In some of our recipes, we say to spray parchment paper that is placed in the cast iron, and that is perfectly acceptable.

SALT Salt adds flavor to food and is essential when baking with yeast, as it strengthens the gluten and regulates the yeast.

It seems that the salt section of the grocery store is now full of various jars, bags and boxes of salt, so which should you use? In this book, recipes that call for just "salt" are referring to table salt. For those that require kosher salt, it is noted accordingly. But what is the difference, and what happens if you don't have one or the other?

Table salt is fine in texture, dissolves quickly and disperses easily in dry ingredients. However, its taste is often described as somewhat chemical. Kosher salt has larger crystals and typically no additives. The larger crystals are especially good for seasoning meat, and chefs have long used it in savory dishes. It is often used for baking.

When comparing 1 tsp (5 mL) of the various kinds of salt, the larger crystals of kosher salt trap more air, so 1 tsp (5 mL) kosher salt will weigh a little less and taste less salty than the same amount of table salt. Within the world of kosher salt, there are two major brands — Diamond Crystal and Morton — and they taste different. We prefer

Diamond Crystal, which is what we used when testing the recipes in this book. Of these two major brands, the same amount of Morton salt will taste much saltier than Diamond Crystal. This means that 2 tsp (10 mL) Diamond Crystal kosher salt equals about 1 tsp (5 mL) Morton kosher salt.

If you have only table salt or one brand of kosher salt, use what you have on hand and adjust the salt level to your personal preference.

SUGAR Granulated sugar is a mainstay for baking. Sugar makes baked goods more tender, adds flavor and browns the surface. We have not tested the recipes using sugar substitutes or sweeteners, but you will find that these replacements will affect the texture and flavor.

For brown sugar, the recipes specify dark brown sugar, but you may choose light or dark — both perform well (the dark has a little more molasses flavor). It seems that many times we choose the one we are most familiar with, so if Roxanne shops for us, she chooses dark, while Kathy chooses light. Brown sugar can be stored at room temperature if kept tightly sealed in an airtight container. Watch for sales before the holidays and stock up.

Coarse white sparkling sugar, sometimes called sanding sugar, decorator sugar or pearl sugar, is a coarse sugar often used as a topping on baked goods. It does not melt as readily as typical granulated sugar, so the baking ends up with a sparkly top and a little texture. If your grocery store does not carry it, look for it at cake-decorating or candy supply shops, craft stores and kitchen and gourmet shops, or through specialty mail-order baking companies.

If you do not have white sparkling sugar, you can substitute turbinado sugar, a natural sugar that is also coarse. Since turbinado is amber to brown in color, it will not have the sparkling white appearance of decorator sugar, but it will still add sweetness and crunch. Turbinado sugar's darker look is something to consider when sprinkling on paler baked products such as scones.

VANILLA We choose real vanilla extract, not imitation, for the best flavor.

YEAST Yeast may seem magical to some people. We find that some students in our classes love baking and experimenting with bread, while others hesitate. There is no mystery! Once you get used to it and remember a couple of tips, it is easy to bake with yeast.

Yeast is a microscopic living organism — a fungus, to be exact. Just like any living thing, if you feed yeast and keep it warm, it grows. As it grows, it produces carbon dioxide, which gets trapped in the strands of gluten in the dough, so the bread rises, very much like what happens when you blow up a balloon. There are two common types of yeast for baking:

Quick-rising (instant) yeast is the one we frequently use. It is easy to work with, as you can add it to the flour and then pour in liquid. It does not have to be dissolved in warm water, a step often called "proofing," before using. Once mixed, the dough will rise more quickly than a dough made with other kinds of yeast.

The liquid to be stirred into the flour is best heated to 120°F to 130°F (49°C to 54°C). This will not feel hot but will be warm to the touch. One exception to this is slow-rise breads, which rise for 12 or up to 24 hours. For those breads, we use room-temperature tap water or water that is just barely warm to the touch, not exceeding 100°F (38°C).

Active dry yeast should be dissolved in warm water before adding it to flour. Check the label on your package, as the ideal temperature varies a little by brand; generally it is between 100°F and 115°F (38°C to 46°C). This water is lukewarm and will barely feel warm.

The most accurate way to ensure that liquid is at the correct temperature is to use an instant-read thermometer. We understand that Grandma's hands may be fine-tuned to checking the temperature with just a touch of her finger, but why risk ruining the bread with liquid that's the wrong temperature when a quick check with an instant-read thermometer will guarantee the right temperature? You can heat the liquid in the microwave or on the stove, but always check the temperature before using it to be sure it is correct.

One $\frac{1}{4}$ oz (7 g) packet of yeast, either quick-rising (instant) or active dry, contains $2\frac{1}{4}$ tsp (11 mL) dry yeast. You can purchase jars and larger packages of yeast instead of the single-use packets. If you begin to bake cast-iron yeast breads frequently, it is wise to purchase the jar or larger package and measure out the amount needed. The amount of yeast required in bread recipes varies and often doesn't equal the amount in one small packet, so we find it easier and less wasteful to use the jars and large packages.

Yeast is perishable, so pay attention to the date on the label for best results. We store all our yeast in the refrigerator. Once a package is opened, transfer it to a container that can be tightly sealed. Typically yeast will stay fresh in the refrigerator for up to 4 months. For longer storage, it can be stored in the freezer for up to 6 months.

Skills and Know-How

BAKING YEAST BREADS

Welcome to baking yeast breads. What is the best part? The unbeatable flavor, the tantalizing aroma, the memories and traditions you are building with your family? Or could it be all of these? In no time, you will be an expert.

In this book, there are two general types of yeast bread: no-knead and kneaded.

NO-KNEAD BREADS

No-knead artisan breads taste great and have a distinctive chewy crust — and they couldn't be easier to make. By "artisan," we mean fresh, homemade breads with a rustic look. They are a little different to make than the more traditional kneaded breads and the dough is quite a bit stickier.

- The dough for no-knead breads is shaggy and loose and sometimes looks almost like a thick batter. Do not be tempted to add additional flour. The high volume of water in this dough allows the gluten to develop so that kneading is not required.

- The water temperature for no-knead bread is not as critical as for baking a kneaded bread. Use room-temperature tap water or just barely warm water.

- After rising, the dough will be spongy. Do not punch it down as you might with a kneaded bread, as you want to retain all the trapped air.

- Place the empty Dutch oven in the oven and preheat for about 30 minutes. Even if the oven heats up more quickly, leave the Dutch oven inside for 30 minutes to be sure it is heated through evenly.

- When baking, do not peek before the first baking time is up.

- If your Dutch oven has a smooth lid with no handles, you can turn the pot upside down and use it like a French cloche, which is a bell-shaped stoneware dome used for baking bread. The lid will become the "skillet" and the rest of the Dutch oven will act as a high-domed cover. Follow recipes as directed.

KNEADED YEAST BREADS

Kneaded yeast breads are warm, inviting and prized for a tender crust and moist interior. Now, with the use of a stand mixer equipped with a dough hook, you can easily knead dough. But do not shy away from kneading by hand; many cooks, including us, describe it as fun and often relaxing. The feel of the warm dough and the rhythmic movements lead to a few moments of quiet, a time to pray or meditate, and gratitude that you are creating a nourishing food for those you love.

- The temperature of the liquid used for this dough is important. For quick-rising (instant) yeast that is added to the flour, the liquid should be heated to between 120°F and 130°F (49°C and 54°C). This will not feel hot but will be warm to the touch. Active dry yeast, which is dissolved in warm water before adding to the flour, requires liquid that is lukewarm — just barely warm to the touch — generally between 100°F and 115°F (38°C and 46°C). Use an instant-read thermometer to check the temperature of the liquid.

- The quantity of flour listed for most bread recipes is approximate. The brand of flour, the humidity in the kitchen, how long the flour has been stored and other factors affect the exact amount needed. But do not overdo the flour: too much will make a heavy bread.

- Do not overdo the amount of flour on your work surface. A sticky dough will often make a better bread.

- To knead by hand, place the dough on a floured work surface. With floured hands, press the dough away from you with the heels of your hands. Fold the dough over, rotate it a quarter-turn and repeat, again pushing it away from you with your hands.

- The recipes in this book will state whether to knead by hand or by using the dough hook on a stand mixer. Generally, if the recipe says to knead with a mixer and dough hook, you can switch and knead the dough by hand on a floured surface. If kneading with your mixer, follow the manufacturer's directions for attaching the dough hook, the volume of dough that can be kneaded and other specific recommendations.

- To test if the dough is fully kneaded, press it with your finger. The dough will spring back if it's ready. Another way is to tear off a small piece and stretch it with your fingers. If the dough tears, knead some more. If it stretches and pulls apart without tearing (the strands are often described as making a windowpane), you have kneaded enough. It is hard to knead too much if you are kneading by hand.

- Grease a large bowl with vegetable oil. Place the ball of dough in the bowl and turn it over to lightly oil it on all sides.

- Cover the bowl of dough with a towel or plastic wrap. Grandma may have used a special towel to cover the dough, but today we often use plastic wrap instead. This helps to keep the humidity up (a good thing). If using a towel, choose a thin woven cotton towel, sometimes called a flour-sack towel or tea towel. Do not use a heavy, absorbent terry-cloth towel.

What Is a Warm, Draft-Free Place?

A warm place will help your bread to rise properly. There are several options to create the ideal temperature that will encourage your dough to rise. Choose the method that is the most convenient for you:

- Today, many ovens have a "proof" cycle that is perfectly calibrated to create a warm environment.

- A gas oven with a pilot light may feel slightly warm and be an ideal place.

- Preheat your oven to 150°F (70°C) or the lowest temperature you can for a few moments. Before putting in the dough, be sure to turn off the oven and double-check that it feels just warm.

- Place a bowl of warm water on the bottom rack of the oven and set the bowl of dough on the rack above it. The warmth from the water will make the oven warm.

- Fill a microwave-safe glass bowl with water, then microwave on High until the water boils. Carefully remove the bowl and place your bowl of dough in the empty microwave oven and close the door.

- The kitchen on a warm day may be just the ideal temperature.

How Can You Tell If Kneaded Bread Dough Has Risen Enough?

If the dough holds the indention from your finger, it is ready to punch down and shape.

Sweeter doughs take longer to rise than bread doughs with little sugar. Do not be surprised if, after an hour, a sweeter dough hardly appears to have risen. Just keep it in a warm spot and give it more time.

Is the Bread Done?

Follow the baking recommendations in the recipes. For both kneaded and no-knead breads, bake until they are golden brown. If the loaf is pale, bake it a little longer. If you pick up the bread carefully, the bottom will also be golden brown and it will sound hollow when tapped with your fingers. Use these cues but, if in doubt, it is probably wise to bake the bread a little longer.

SLICING AND STORING BREAD

As tempting as it is to cut a slice of warm bread, if will be gummy if sliced while too hot. Allow the loaf to cool on a wire rack before slicing. To slice by hand, use a sharp serrated bread knife. If it's very crusty, you might find that an electric knife or even a home food slicer is a convenient tool. But, of course, there are times when we cut bread warm to go with a meal, such as to make the best accompaniment for a bowl of soup.

Once completely cool, place the bread in a muslin bread bag or wrap it in parchment paper for storage. Breads with crispy, chewy crusts will lose that texture if placed in a plastic bag or airtight container. Kneaded breads with softer crusts and sweet rolls can be stored in an airtight container or bag.

These breads are baked without preservatives, so for best flavor, enjoy them the day they are baked or within a day or two. Bread will taste stale if stored in the refrigerator. For longer storage, place the loaf in a resealable freezer bag and freeze for up to 6 months. For us it is most convenient to slice the bread before freezing, so it is easy to pull out a slice or two when needed.

TIPS FOR BISCUITS, SCONES AND PIE CRUSTS

- Cutting in cold butter is a common step when baking biscuits, scones and pie crusts. To do this, use a pastry blender or two knives in an up-and-down motion to cut the butter into tiny pieces, forming coarse crumbs that we describe as "pea-size." Fingertips are a convenient alternative to a pastry blender: use your thumb and fingers to rub the butter into the flour, using a snapping motion.

- The liquid amount for each recipe is approximate and will vary. Add the liquid (ice water, milk, buttermilk or cream) and blend until the flour is moistened. The moisture content of flour varies, so you may find you need to add an extra bit of liquid to moisten all of the flour. Add the minimum amount of liquid specified, then, if the flour is still dry, drizzle in an additional 1 to 2 tbsp (15 to 30 mL) as needed to moisten the flour.

- Do not overwork or knead the dough for biscuits, scones or pie crusts, as this will toughen them.

- Biscuits are best served the day they are made and taste wonderful warm from the oven. Store leftover biscuits in an airtight container at room temperature for up to 2 days. To reheat, wrap a biscuit in a paper towel and microwave on High for 20 seconds. To freeze, wrap individual baked biscuits tightly and store for up to 2 to 3 months.

Unwrap the number of frozen biscuits you want to serve and arrange them on a rimmed baking sheet (do not thaw). Bake in an oven preheated to 350°F (180°C) for 10 to 15 minutes or until heated through.

CUTTING BISCUITS

To cut biscuits, flour a biscuit cutter or round cookie cutter approximately the size specified in the recipe. If you do not have a cutter, select a glass with a similar sized rim, flour the rim and proceed with the recipe. Do not twist the biscuit cutter; use a quick motion straight downward. Twisting the cutter compresses the edges of the biscuits so they do not rise as high.

TIPS FOR PIES

- Ice-cold water is used for pie crusts. When we make pie crusts, the first thing we do is pour cold water over a cup of ice so it is icy cold and ready to use when needed. If the water is too warm, the fat in the recipe may melt and coat the flour. Ice water keeps the bits of fat intact, which helps makes the crust flaky.

- Wrap prepared pie crust in plastic wrap and refrigerate until chilled, at least 30 minutes or up to 3 days. For longer storage, freeze and use within 6 to 8 weeks. Thaw in the refrigerator overnight. Note: While some references suggest rolling the pastry and putting it in the pie pan before freezing, you should not freeze a cast-iron skillet. We also find that if pie crust has been refrigerated for 2 or more hours and is very cold, you may need to set it out at room temperature for about 30 minutes prior to baking, so that it can be rolled out easily.

- You can substitute store-bought refrigerated pie crust. Roll out the crust until it is thin and about 12 inches (30 cm) in diameter.

- In the recipes in this book, we suggest rolling out the crust on a lightly floured work surface using a floured rolling pin. Loosely fold the rolled dough into quarters and transfer it to the cast-iron skillet. As an alternative method, gently roll the pastry circle onto the rolling pin, then gently unroll it into the skillet. Do not pull or stretch the dough, for this will cause it to shrink and become misshapen while baking.

- If baking a pie crust empty (blind), place the pastry in the skillet, then use a fork to prick the bottom all over. Bake the crust at 425°F (220°C) for 10 to 12 minutes or until lightly brown.

- If adapting your favorite pie recipe to a cast-iron skillet, you may need to prepare 1½ times the filling amount, as a skillet is deep. Typically a pie made in a cast-iron skillet serves 12.

- After serving, do not store leftovers in the cast-iron skillet. A fruit pie can sit at room temperature for a day, then should be refrigerated. Cream or custard pies should be refrigerated after serving. To remove leftover pie from the skillet, cut the pie in half, then slide a wide, flat spatula under the crust and check to be sure it is loosened. Gently lift the pie out of the skillet and place on a platter. Repeat with the remaining half.

TIPS FOR PIZZA AND FLATBREADS

We often use our fingertips instead of a rolling pin when flattening dough to the correct thickness for pizza or flatbread. Once the dough is ready to be shaped, flatten it with your hands into a 6-inch (15 cm) circle. Hold the edges of the dough in the air and then, as you rotate the circle, stretch and lengthen it to a 10-inch (25 cm) diameter. It may be easier (and it certainly is acceptable) to use a floured rolling pin to roll the dough into a 10-inch (25 cm) circle.

TIPS FOR COOKIES AND BROWNIES

Do you want chewy brownies or are you a fan of more cakelike bar cookies? The cast-iron skillet does it all, and sometimes you may find you get both textures in one batch. There is always someone who prefers extra-crisp cookies, and those pieces will be along the outer edge, while the chewy portions will be in the middle.

For chewy or fudgy cookies, take the cast-iron skillet out of the oven after the minimum baking time. For firmer cookies, use the maximum baking time. Remember, thanks to the residual heat of cast iron, the food will continue to bake when removed from the oven.

Cut the cookies or brownies as you prefer. Sometimes a wedge is ideal, while at other times we prefer to cut skillet cookies or brownies into 2-inch (5 cm) squares. One benefit of the square is that people can select a small piece from either the crispy edge or the chewier center. However, with wedges, everyone can enjoy both the crispy edges and the chewier center. Both are delicious.

SLOW-RISE BREADS

Artisan No-Knead Bread

MAKES 1 LOAF

This is the recipe that began our love of cast-iron baking. Over the course of the COVID-19 pandemic, we have baked hundreds of loaves of no-knead bread between us. It really can't be any easier: all you do is stir the ingredients together, let the dough rest on the kitchen counter for 12 to 18 hours, and then bake until you have a crispy, deeply flavored loaf. We like to toast slices of the bread, then spread with butter and jam, but it is also perfect for paninis and grilled cheese sandwiches.

5-quart (4.7 L) cast-iron Dutch oven with lid

3 cups (750 mL) all-purpose flour (approx.)

½ cup (125 mL) whole wheat flour

1 tbsp (15 mL) kosher salt

½ tsp (2 mL) quick-rising (instant) yeast

1⅔ cups (400 mL) water (approx.)

1 In a large bowl, combine all-purpose flour, whole wheat flour, salt and yeast. Add water and stir until combined. The dough should be shaggy and sticky, so add an additional 1 to 2 tbsp (15 to 30 mL) water if it is too dry. Cover with plastic wrap and let rise at room temperature for at least 12 hours or preferably 18 hours.

2 Place dough on a lightly floured work surface. Sprinkle with flour and fold the dough over onto itself once or twice. Lightly flour a 15-inch (38 cm) square of parchment paper. Place dough on parchment paper, cover with plastic wrap and let stand for at least 15 minutes or up to 30 minutes.

3 Meanwhile, place the covered Dutch oven in the oven and preheat to 450°F (230°C).

4 Carefully lift parchment paper with the dough into the hot Dutch oven. Cover with lid and bake for 30 minutes. Remove lid and continue to bake for an additional 18 to 20 minutes or until brown and crisp.

5 Remove Dutch oven and place on a wire rack. Carefully, using a heatproof spatula, lift bread out of the Dutch oven and place on a wire rack. Cool, then slice and serve.

No-Knead Honey Bread

This no-knead, easy-peasy recipe is a sweeter version of a no-knead bread and ideal for peanut butter and jelly sandwiches. You may think you have outgrown such a treat, but one bite of this bread and you will be transported to your elementary school lunchroom. PB&Js just not your thing? This makes equally delicious deli sandwiches and turns lunchtime into a high point of your day.

10-inch (25 cm) cast-iron skillet

2½ cups (625 mL) all-purpose flour (approx.)

½ cup (125 mL) whole wheat flour

2 tsp (10 mL) kosher salt

½ tsp (2 mL) quick-rising (instant) yeast

1½ cups (375 mL) water (approx.)

1 tbsp (15 mL) liquid honey

1 tbsp (15 mL) unsalted butter, melted

1 In a large bowl, combine all-purpose flour, whole wheat flour, salt and yeast. Add water, honey and melted butter and stir until combined. The dough should be shaggy and sticky, so add an additional 1 to 2 tbsp (15 to 30 mL) water if it is too dry. Cover with plastic wrap and let rise at room temperature for 12 hours or preferably 18 hours.

2 Place dough on a lightly floured work surface. Sprinkle with flour and fold the dough over onto itself 3 times. Lightly flour a 15-inch (38 cm) square of parchment paper. Shape dough into a ball, then place on the parchment paper. Cover with plastic wrap and let stand for at least 15 minutes or up to 30 minutes.

3 Meanwhile, place skillet in the oven and preheat to 450°F (230°C).

4 Carefully lift parchment paper with the dough into the hot skillet. Bake, uncovered, for 35 to 40 minutes or until brown.

5 Remove skillet from the oven and place on a wire rack. Using a heatproof spatula, transfer bread to a wire rack. Cool, then slice and serve.

Gluten-Free Bread

MAKES 1 LOAF

No need to think that a gluten-free diet will sideline you from enjoying a slice of crusty bread. Thanks to the gluten-free flour blends now available, you can easily make this tasty bread at home.

Electric mixer

5-quart (4.7 L) cast-iron Dutch oven with lid

3¼ cups (810 mL) all-purpose gluten-free flour (approx.; see Tip)

2 tbsp (30 mL) flax seeds, divided

1 tbsp (15 mL) packed brown sugar

1½ tsp (7 mL) kosher salt

1½ tsp (7 mL) quick-rising (instant) yeast

1¾ cups (425 mL) tepid water (90°F to 100°F/32°C to 38°C), approx.

1 tbsp (15 mL) coarse-ground yellow cornmeal

1 In a large bowl, combine flour, 1 tbsp (15 mL) flax seeds, brown sugar, salt and yeast. Stir in the water. Using an electric mixer, beat at medium speed for 1 minute. (The mixture will make a sticky batter. It will thicken slightly as it stands, so do not be tempted to add additional flour.)

2 Cover with plastic wrap and let rise at room temperature for 1 hour, then transfer to the refrigerator for 24 hours.

3 Line a basket or bowl, about 8 to 9 inches (20 to 23 cm) in diameter, with a 15-inch (38 cm) square of parchment paper. Lightly flour the paper. Gently spoon batter onto the parchment paper, retaining as much of the leaven (rise) as possible. Sprinkle the top of the batter with the remaining flax seeds and the cornmeal. Cover with plastic wrap and let stand for 30 minutes.

4 Meanwhile, place the covered Dutch oven in the oven and preheat to 450°F (230°C).

5 Carefully lift parchment paper with the dough into the hot Dutch oven. Cover with lid and bake for 30 minutes. Remove lid and continue to bake for an additional 10 to 15 minutes or until brown and crisp.

6 Remove Dutch oven and place on a wire rack. Carefully, using a heatproof spatula, transfer bread to a wire rack. Cool, then slice and serve.

> **TIP** | There are many blends of all-purpose gluten-free flour today. Some brands contain xanthan gum, a common food additive that binds ingredients and adds volume, while others do not. Make sure to check the label. If the gluten-free flour you are using does not contain xanthan gum, add 1¾ tsp (8 mL) xanthan gum to the flour mixture in Step 1. It will help the dough to rise and create a lighter loaf. If xanthan gum is not available or you prefer not to add it, this bread will taste fine but the shape and texture will be more compact. Look for xanthan gum at well-stocked grocery stores, health food stores or online.

Everyday Whole-Grain Bread

MAKES 1 LOAF

With a recipe this easy, you really can enjoy whole-grain bread every day! Don't be surprised that all-purpose flour is used here; many whole-grain breads contain a small amount to help create structure so the dough rises, and this one is no exception. The bread will be denser than those made completely with all-purpose flour, but this delectable wheat loaf, which contains rolled oats and a dusting of cornmeal and wheat germ, will deliver nutritious whole-grain benefits with a delicious nutty flavor.

5-quart (4.7 L) cast-iron Dutch oven with lid

2 cups (500 mL) whole wheat flour

¾ cup (175 mL) all-purpose flour (approx.)

2 tsp (10 mL) kosher salt

2 tsp (10 mL) packed dark brown sugar

1½ tsp (7 mL) quick-rising (instant) yeast

1⅔ cups (400 mL) tepid water (90°F to 100°F/32°C to 38°C), approx.

¼ cup (60 mL) large-flake (old-fashioned) rolled oats

1 tbsp (15 mL) wheat germ

1 tbsp (15 mL) coarse-ground yellow cornmeal

1 In a large bowl, combine whole wheat flour, all-purpose flour, salt, brown sugar and yeast. Add water and stir until combined. The dough should be shaggy and sticky, so add an additional 1 to 2 tbsp (15 to 30 mL) water if it is too dry. Stir in the oats. Cover with plastic wrap and let rise at room temperature for at least 18 hours or preferably 24 hours.

2 Lightly flour a 15-inch (38 cm) square of parchment paper. Place dough on parchment paper, sprinkle with flour and, using floured fingertips, fold the dough onto itself once or twice. Shape the dough into a ball. Sprinkle with wheat germ and cornmeal. Cover with plastic wrap. Let stand for 45 minutes.

3 Meanwhile, place the covered Dutch oven in the oven and preheat to 450°F (230°C).

4 Using a sharp knife, slash the top of the dough. Carefully lift the parchment paper with the dough into the hot Dutch oven. Cover with lid and bake for 30 minutes. Remove lid and continue to bake for an additional 15 to 20 minutes or until brown and crisp.

5 Remove Dutch oven and place on a wire rack. Carefully, using a heatproof spatula, transfer bread to a wire rack. Cool, then slice and serve.

> **TIP** | If desired, substitute white whole wheat flour (a specialty whole wheat flour that is lighter in color and milder in flavor) or even regular whole wheat flour for some of the all-purpose flour. Since whole-grain bread is denser than breads made with all-purpose flour, using more whole-grain flour will result in a bread that rises less. Experiment a little to determine the flavor and texture you prefer.

Cinnamon Raisin No-Knead Bread

MAKES 1 LOAF

The name of this bread may sound classic and somewhat modest, but one taste will change your perception — it is truly divine. The raisins are stirred into the dough; then, while the dough rises, the flavor permeates the bread. What an incredible treat!

5-quart (4.7 L) cast-iron Dutch oven with lid

3 cups (750 mL) all-purpose flour (approx.)

3 tbsp (45 mL) granulated sugar

2 tsp (10 mL) ground cinnamon

1½ tsp (7 mL) kosher salt

¾ tsp (3 mL) quick-rising (instant) yeast

¾ cup (175 mL) dark raisins

1½ cups (375 mL) water (approx.)

1 In a large bowl, combine flour, sugar, cinnamon, salt and yeast. Stir in raisins. Add water and stir until combined. The dough should be shaggy and sticky, so add an additional 1 to 2 tbsp (15 to 30 mL) water if it is too dry. Cover with plastic wrap and let rise at room temperature for at least 12 hours or preferably 18 hours.

2 Place dough on a lightly floured work surface. Sprinkle lightly with flour and fold the dough over onto itself 3 times. Lightly flour a 15-inch (38 cm) square of parchment paper. Shape dough into a ball, then place on parchment paper. Cover with plastic wrap and let stand for 30 minutes.

3 Meanwhile, place the covered Dutch oven in the oven and preheat to 450°F (230°C).

4 Carefully lift parchment paper with the dough into the hot Dutch oven. Cover with lid and bake for 30 minutes. Remove lid and continue to bake for an additional 10 to 15 minutes or until brown and crisp.

5 Remove Dutch oven and place on a wire rack. Carefully, using a heatproof spatula, transfer bread to a wire rack. Cool, then slice and serve.

VARIATION

CRANBERRY WALNUT NO-KNEAD BREAD
Substitute sweetened dried cranberries for the raisins and add ½ cup (125 mL) chopped walnuts along with the cranberries. Proceed with the recipe as directed.

No-Knead Rosemary Bread

MAKES 1 LOAF

This bread is the perfect accompaniment for a cheese board and equally delicious for building sandwiches the next day.

5-quart (4.7 L) cast-iron Dutch oven with lid

2½ cups (625 mL) all-purpose flour (approx.)

½ cup (125 mL) whole wheat flour

2 tsp (10 mL) kosher salt

½ tsp (2 mL) quick-rising (instant) yeast

1 tbsp (15 mL) finely chopped fresh rosemary

3 garlic cloves, minced

1½ cups (375 mL) water (approx.)

1 tbsp (15 mL) olive oil

1 In a large bowl, combine all-purpose flour, whole wheat flour, salt, yeast, rosemary and garlic. Add water and oil; stir until combined. The dough should be shaggy and sticky, so add an additional 1 to 2 tbsp (15 to 30 mL) water if needed. Cover with plastic wrap and let rise at room temperature for 12 hours or preferably 18 hours.

2 Place dough on a lightly floured work surface. Sprinkle with flour and fold the dough over onto itself 3 times. Lightly flour a 15-inch (38 cm) square of parchment paper. Shape dough into a ball, then place on the parchment paper. Cover with plastic wrap and let stand for at least 15 minutes or up to 30 minutes.

3 Meanwhile, place the covered Dutch oven in the oven and preheat to 450°F (230°C).

4 Carefully lift parchment paper with the dough into the hot Dutch oven. Cover with lid and bake for 30 minutes. Remove lid and continue to bake for an additional 18 to 20 minutes or until brown and crisp.

5 Remove Dutch oven and place on a wire rack. Carefully, using a heatproof spatula, transfer bread to a wire rack. Cool, then slice and serve.

FLATBREADS AND PIZZA

Focaccia with Onion and Sun-Dried Tomatoes

MAKES ONE 10-INCH (25 CM) FOCACCIA

This is an ideal focaccia bread to serve on Saturday evening when friends come over, since it's both flavorful and impressive. Everyone can enjoy a slice with a cocktail or a glass of wine.

Stand mixer

10-inch (25 cm) cast-iron skillet

2½ cups (625 mL) all-purpose flour (approx.), divided

1½ tsp (7 mL) quick-rising (instant) yeast

1½ tsp (7 mL) granulated sugar

1½ tsp (7 mL) kosher salt

1 cup (250 mL) warm water (120°F to 130°F/49°C to 54°C)

3 tbsp + ¼ tsp (46 mL) olive oil, divided

ONION AND SUN-DRIED TOMATO TOPPING

1 tbsp (15 mL) olive oil

1 sweet onion, thinly sliced

2 garlic cloves, minced

1 tsp (5 mL) minced fresh basil leaves

1 tsp (5 mL) minced fresh thyme leaves

½ tsp (2 mL) kosher salt

¼ cup (60 mL) oil-packed sun-dried tomatoes, drained (with oil reserved) and sliced

1 In the bowl of the stand mixer fitted with the paddle attachment, combine 1½ cups (375 mL) flour, yeast, sugar and salt. Add warm water and 3 tbsp (45 mL) oil. Beat at medium speed for 1 minute. Stir in remaining 1 cup (250 mL) flour to make a soft dough. If dough is very sticky, stir in an additional 2 to 4 tbsp (30 to 60 mL) flour. Replace paddle attachment with the dough hook. Knead until dough is smooth and springs back when pressed lightly with a finger, about 5 minutes.

2 Lightly grease a large bowl with the remaining ¼ tsp (1 mL) oil. With lightly floured hands, shape dough into a ball, place in the bowl and turn to coat the top. Cover with a clean dish towel and let rise in a warm, draft-free place for about 1 hour or until doubled in size.

3 ONION AND SUN-DRIED TOMATO TOPPING Meanwhile, heat oil in the skillet over medium heat. Add onion and cook, stirring frequently, until tender and golden brown, about 10 minutes. Stir in garlic and cook until fragrant, about 30 seconds. Spoon onion and garlic into a bowl; add basil, thyme and salt. Let skillet cool for 15 minutes, then wipe clean (it does not need to cool completely). Set topping aside.

4 Meanwhile, preheat the oven to 425°F (220°C). Punch down dough and let stand for 10 minutes. Pat dough evenly into the clean skillet, pressing to the edges. Using fingertips, make depressions ½ inch (1 cm) deep and about 2 inches (5 cm) apart over the surface of the dough. Brush 2 tbsp (30 mL) reserved sun-dried tomato oil lightly over the dough. Discard remaining oil.

5 Bake in the preheated oven for 10 minutes. Remove skillet from the oven and place on a wire rack. Scatter tomatoes over the bread. Spoon onion mixture over the tomatoes. Bake for 20 to 25 minutes more or until golden brown.

6 Remove skillet from the oven and place on a wire rack. Let cool for 5 minutes. Cut focaccia into pieces and serve warm from the skillet.

Rosemary Focaccia Bread

MAKES ONE 10-INCH (25 CM) FOCACCIA

The best focaccia are a little chewy and have a depth of flavor that develops during the rising time, and one way to achieve both is to make the dough the day ahead. This dough rises in the refrigerator, so it is ready to bake the next day.

Stand mixer

10-inch (25 cm) cast-iron skillet

2½ cups (625 mL) all-purpose flour (approx.), divided

1¼ tsp (6 mL) granulated sugar

1¼ tsp (6 mL) kosher salt

1 tsp (5 mL) quick-rising (instant) yeast

1¼ cups (310 mL) warm water (120°F to 130°F/49°C to 54°C)

3 tbsp + ¼ tsp (46 mL) olive oil, divided

ROSEMARY TOPPING

1½ tbsp (22 mL) olive oil

2 garlic cloves, minced

2 tbsp (30 mL) minced fresh rosemary

½ tsp (2 mL) kosher salt

¼ tsp (1 mL) freshly ground black pepper

1 In the bowl of the stand mixer fitted with the paddle attachment, combine 2 cups (500 mL) flour, sugar, salt and yeast. Add warm water and 2 tbsp (30 mL) oil. Beat at medium-high speed for 2 minutes.

2 Stir in the remaining ½ cup (125 mL) flour to form a soft dough. If the dough seems very sticky, add an additional 2 to 3 tbsp (30 to 45 mL) flour.

3 Lightly grease a large bowl with ¼ tsp (1 mL) oil. With lightly floured hands, gather dough into a sticky ball. Place dough in the bowl and turn to coat the top. Cover with plastic wrap and refrigerate for 18 to 24 hours.

4 Preheat the oven to 450°F (230°C).

5 Drizzle remaining 1 tbsp (15 mL) oil into the skillet and swirl to coat. Add the dough. With wet fingertips, pat dough evenly into the skillet, pressing to the edges. Using fingertips, make depressions ½ inch (1 cm) deep and about 2 inches (5 cm) apart in the surface of the dough. Cover with plastic wrap. Let stand at room temperature for 15 minutes.

6 **ROSEMARY TOPPING** Meanwhile, in a small bowl, combine oil, garlic, rosemary, salt and pepper. Lightly brush topping over the focaccia.

7 Bake in the preheated oven for 20 to 25 minutes or until golden brown. Remove the skillet from the oven and place on a wire rack. Let cool for 5 minutes. Cut focaccia into pieces and serve warm from the skillet.

VARIATION

ROSEMARY THYME FOCACCIA BREAD Prepare the bread as directed. Add 2 tsp (10 mL) minced fresh thyme leaves to the topping in Step 6. Proceed with the recipe as directed.

One-Hour Skillet Focaccia

MAKES ONE 10-INCH (25 CM) FOCACCIA

Warm herbed flatbread can be a quick addition to any meal, even on those busy weeknights when dinnertime becomes a time crunch. From the mixing bowl to warm on your plate, this flatbread can be ready to serve in an hour.

10-inch (25 cm) cast-iron skillet

2 cups (500 mL) all-purpose flour, divided

1¾ tsp (8 mL) quick-rising (instant) yeast

1½ tsp (7 mL) kosher salt

1 tsp (5 mL) granulated sugar

¾ cup (175 mL) warm water (120°F to 130°F/49°C to 54°C)

2 tbsp + 1 tsp (35 mL) olive oil, divided

GARLIC-HERB TOPPING

1 tbsp (15 mL) olive oil

2 garlic cloves, minced

1 tsp (5 mL) Italian seasoning

¼ tsp (1 mL) kosher salt

2 tbsp (30 mL) freshly grated Parmesan cheese

1 In a large bowl, combine 1 cup (250 mL) flour, yeast, salt and sugar. Add warm water and 2 tbsp (30 mL) oil; stir vigorously until batter is smooth. Add remaining 1 cup (250 mL) flour and stir vigorously until it forms a sticky dough.

2 Grease skillet with the remaining 1 tsp (5 mL) oil. Transfer dough to the skillet. With wet fingertips, pat dough evenly into the skillet, pressing to the edges. Using fingertips, make depressions ½ inch (1 cm) deep and about 2 inches (5 cm) apart over the surface of the dough. Cover with a clean dish towel. Let stand at room temperature for 20 minutes.

3 Preheat the oven to 400°F (200°C).

4 **GARLIC-HERB TOPPING** In a small bowl, combine oil, garlic, Italian seasoning and salt. Lightly brush the topping over the dough.

5 Bake in the preheated oven for 15 minutes. Sprinkle evenly with Parmesan cheese. Bake for 5 to 8 minutes more or until golden brown.

6 Remove skillet from the oven and place on a wire rack. Let cool for 5 minutes. Cut focaccia into pieces and serve warm from the skillet.

Cornbread Focaccia

MAKES ONE 10-INCH (25 CM) FOCACCIA

Cornbread focaccia has a delightful texture and flavor. We like to slice this bread into sandwich-size squares and then cut each square in half horizontally. Pile the bread high with your favorite deli meats and cheeses for sandwiches that elevate ho-hum lunches into an all-time favorite. It's a great idea for picnics in the park, too.

10-inch (25 cm) cast-iron skillet

1½ tsp (7 mL) quick-rising (instant) yeast

½ tsp (2 mL) granulated sugar

¼ cup + ⅔ cup (210 mL) lukewarm water (100°F to 115°F/38°C to 46°C), divided

1 tbsp + ¼ tsp (16 mL) olive oil

1 tsp (5 mL) salt

2 cups (500 mL) all-purpose flour (approx.)

½ cup (125 mL) coarse-ground yellow cornmeal

TOPPINGS

1 tbsp (15 mL) olive oil

1 garlic clove, minced

½ tsp (2 mL) Italian seasoning

8 grape or cherry tomatoes, cut in half

⅓ cup (75 mL) freshly grated Parmesan cheese

¼ tsp (1 mL) kosher salt

1 In a large bowl, combine yeast, sugar and ¼ cup (60 mL) lukewarm water. Let stand for 5 minutes. Add remaining ⅔ cup (150 mL) water, 1 tbsp (15 mL) oil and salt. Stir in the flour and cornmeal to form a soft dough.

2 Place the dough on a lightly floured work surface and knead for about 8 minutes or until dough is smooth and springs back when pressed lightly with a finger.

3 Lightly grease a large bowl with ¼ tsp (1 mL) oil. Place dough in the bowl and turn to coat the top. Cover with a clean dish towel and let rise in a warm, draft-free place for about 1 hour or until doubled in size. The dough is ready when an indentation remains after pressing with a finger.

4 **TOPPINGS** Meanwhile, in a small bowl, combine oil and garlic. Set aside.

5 Preheat the oven to 425°F (220°C).

6 Punch down dough and place in skillet. Pat dough evenly into the skillet, pressing to the edges. Using fingertips, make depressions ½ inch (1 cm) deep and about 2 inches (5 cm) apart over the surface of the dough. Brush the oil-garlic mixture over the dough. Sprinkle the dough evenly with Italian seasoning. Gently press tomato halves, cut side down, evenly into depressions in the dough. Sprinkle evenly with Parmesan cheese and salt.

7 Bake in the preheated oven for 20 to 25 minutes or until golden brown and cheese has melted.

8 Remove skillet from the oven and place on a wire rack. Let cool for 5 minutes. Serve focaccia warm or at room temperature.

Cast-Iron Weeknight Pizza

MAKES ONE 10-INCH (25 CM) THICK-CRUST PIZZA

Who wouldn't want hot, cheesy, savory and chewy pizza baked in your own oven, with no more fussing and fretting over a delayed pizza delivery on a Friday night? This recipe gives you a lot of flexibility to create your own masterpiece. However, make sure not to overload the pizza with more than four toppings, to allow the crust to bake perfectly.

10-inch (25 cm) cast-iron skillet

½ cup (125 mL) warm water (120°F to 130°F/49°C to 54°C)

1¼ tsp (6 mL) quick-rising (instant) yeast

1½ cups (375 mL) all-purpose flour (approx.), divided

1 tbsp + ¼ tsp (16 mL) olive oil, divided

½ tsp (2 mL) kosher salt

½ cup (125 mL) store-bought pizza sauce

1½ cups (375 mL) shredded mozzarella cheese

¼ cup (60 mL) freshly grated Parmesan cheese

OPTIONAL TOPPINGS

Crumbled cooked hot or mild (sweet) Italian sausage

Sliced pepperoni

Crumbled cooked bacon

Sliced white mushrooms

Sliced pitted olives

Chopped onions

Sliced or chopped green pepper

Fresh basil

1 In a large bowl, combine water, yeast and ¾ cup (175 mL) flour; stir until smooth. Add 1 tbsp (15 mL) oil, salt and another ½ cup (125 mL) flour. Stir until a soft dough forms. Sprinkle remaining ¼ cup (60 mL) flour on a work surface. Place dough on the floured surface and knead, incorporating the flour on the work surface into the pizza dough. Continue to knead until the dough is smooth and springs back when pressed lightly with a finger. This will take about 5 to 10 minutes.

2 Lightly grease a medium bowl with remaining ¼ tsp (1 mL) oil. Place dough in the bowl and turn the dough to coat the top. Cover bowl with plastic wrap and let rise until doubled in size, about 1 hour.

3 Meanwhile, preheat the oven to 475°F (240°C).

4 Punch down dough in the bowl. Cover with a clean dish towel and let stand for 10 minutes.

5 Turn dough out on a lightly floured surface and shape into a ball. Flatten dough with your hands into a 6-inch (15 cm) circle. Using a floured rolling pin, roll the dough into a 10-inch (25 cm) circle.

continued on page 54

6 Place dough in the skillet. Spread pizza sauce evenly over the dough. Top with mozzarella cheese, Parmesan cheese and toppings (if using). Bake in the preheated oven for 14 to 16 minutes, until cheese is melted and crust is golden.

7 Remove skillet from the oven and place on a wire rack. Using a heatproof spatula, transfer pizza from the skillet to a wire rack. Let stand for 10 minutes before cutting.

TIP | To make 2 thin-crust pizzas, divide the dough in half at the end of Step 4 and place both on a lightly floured surface. Form each half into a smooth ball. Place one ball in a resealable bag and refrigerate for up 1 week. Use the remaining dough ball to proceed with the recipe as directed, using half the sauce, cheeses and topping for each pizza.

Chicago-Style Pizza

MAKES ONE 10-INCH (25 CM) PIZZA

For more than three decades we have traveled to Chicago to work at the International Home & Housewares Show. No trip would be complete, however, if we didn't stop at Gino's East, just off Michigan Avenue, for some Chicago-style pizza. While we can't hop on a plane every time we crave this deep-dish crust with a hint of cornmeal, we have been able to replicate it at home, thanks to the cast-iron skillet. Now we can enjoy a taste of Chicago anytime we please.

Stand mixer

10-inch (25 cm) cast-iron skillet

3 cups (750 mL) all-purpose flour (approx.)

2 tbsp (30 mL) coarse-ground yellow cornmeal

2 tsp (10 mL) quick-rising (instant) yeast

1 tsp (5 mL) salt

¾ cup + 1 tbsp (190 mL) warm water (120°F to 130°F/49°C to 54°C)

3 tbsp (45 mL) unsalted butter, melted

5 tsp (25 mL) vegetable oil

5¼ tsp (26 mL) olive oil, divided

FILLING

1 can (14 oz/398 mL) diced tomatoes, well drained (see Tip)

2 garlic cloves, minced

1½ tsp (7 mL) Italian seasoning

1 tsp (5 mL) granulated sugar

8 oz (250 g) fresh mozzarella, sliced about ¼ inch (0.5 cm) thick

8 oz (250 g) Italian sausage crumbles, cooked crisp

Sliced pitted black olives (optional)

Sliced white mushrooms (optional)

1 cup (250 mL) freshly grated Parmesan cheese

2 tsp (10 mL) olive oil

1 In the bowl of the stand mixer fitted with the paddle attachment, combine flour, cornmeal, yeast, salt, warm water, melted butter, vegetable oil and 5 tsp (25 mL) olive oil. Beat on medium speed for 5 minutes. Form dough into a ball.

2 Lightly grease a large bowl with the remaining ¼ tsp (1 mL) olive oil. Place dough in the bowl and turn to coat the top. Cover with a clean dish towel and let rise in a warm, draft-free place for about 1 hour or until doubled in size.

3 Punch down dough and turn out onto a lightly floured work surface. Stretch the dough to form a circle about 10 inches (25 cm) in diameter. Place the dough in the skillet and stretch it to reach the edges. Cover with plastic wrap and let stand for 15 minutes.

4 Preheat the oven to 425°F (220°C). Stretch dough again, over the bottom and up the sides of the skillet. Cover with plastic wrap and let stand for 15 minutes.

5 Bake in the preheated oven for 10 minutes.

6 FILLING Meanwhile, in a small bowl, combine tomatoes, garlic, Italian seasoning and sugar. Set aside.

continued on page 57

7 Remove skillet from the oven and place on a wire rack. Using the back of a large spoon, push down the bottom of the crust, leaving it up the sides.

8 Place the mozzarella slices over the bottom of the crust. Evenly add sausage overtop. Add olives and mushrooms (if using). Top with tomato mixture. Sprinkle evenly with Parmesan cheese. Drizzle olive oil overtop. Bake for 25 to 30 minutes or until the filling is bubbling and the crust is golden brown.

9 Remove skillet from the oven and place on a wire rack. Using a heatproof spatula, transfer pizza from the skillet to a wire rack. Let stand for 10 minutes before cutting.

TIP | It is very important that the tomatoes are well drained, or the pizza will become soggy. Place them in a fine-mesh sieve and press with the back of a spoon to remove all excess moisture.

Gluten-Free Pizza

MAKES ONE 10-INCH (25 CM) PIZZA

Gluten-free all-purpose flour forms the basis of this gluten-free crust, but the cast-iron skillet is the secret weapon, which makes it bake up crisp and tasty. Customize this pizza with your favorite pizza sauce and toppings. The crust also happens to be dairy-free, so if you need to avoid both gluten and dairy, top it with your favorite pizza sauce, then add fresh minced herbs and chopped or sliced vegetables.

Electric mixer

10-inch (25 cm) cast-iron skillet lined with a 15-inch (38 cm) square of parchment paper

1½ cups (375 mL) gluten-free all-purpose flour

1 tsp (5 mL) quick-rising (instant) yeast

1 tsp (5 mL) kosher salt

¼ tsp (1 mL) baking powder

½ cup (125 mL) warm water (120°F to 130°F/49°C to 54°C)

3 tbsp (45 mL) olive oil, divided

2 tsp (10 mL) liquid honey

½ cup (125 mL) store-bought pizza sauce

OPTIONAL TOPPINGS

Sliced fresh mozzarella cheese

Freshly grated Parmesan cheese

Sliced pepperoni

Crumbled cooked sausage

Thinly sliced onions

Sliced or chopped green pepper

Sliced white mushrooms

Minced basil

Minced oregano

1 In a large bowl, combine flour, yeast, salt and baking powder. Add warm water, 2 tbsp (30 mL) oil and honey. Beat with an electric mixer at medium speed for 3 minutes. (The batter will be thin but it will thicken slightly as it stands.) Cover with plastic wrap and let stand in a warm, draft-free place for 30 minutes.

2 Meanwhile, preheat the oven to 450°F (230°C).

3 Drizzle the remaining 1 tbsp (15 mL) oil over the parchment paper in the skillet and swirl to coat evenly. Spoon the sticky, thickened batter into the prepared skillet and, using the back of a spoon, spread it evenly across the bottom.

4 Bake in the preheated oven for 8 minutes or until set and lightly brown.

5 Remove the skillet from the oven and place on a wire rack. Spread pizza sauce evenly over the crust. Sprinkle with toppings (if using). Bake for 5 minutes or until toppings are hot and cheese is melted.

6 Remove skillet from the oven and place on a wire rack. Using a heatproof spatula, transfer pizza from the skillet to a wire rack. Let stand for 10 minutes before cutting.

Pizzeria-Style Pizza

MAKES ONE 10-INCH (25 CM) PIZZA

If you have been searching for a crisp pizzeria-style crust at home, search no more. Guaranteed to rival your favorite takeout pizza, with no reason to leave the comfort of your own home!

10-inch (25 cm) cast-iron skillet

¾ cup (175 mL) all-purpose flour (approx.)

3 tbsp (45 mL) whole wheat flour

½ tsp (2 mL) kosher salt

¼ tsp (1 mL) quick-rising (instant) yeast

½ cup (125 mL) water

½ cup (125 mL) store-bought pizza sauce

OPTIONAL TOPPINGS

Sliced fresh mozzarella cheese

Freshly grated Parmesan cheese

Crumbled cooked hot or mild (sweet) Italian sausage

Sliced pepperoni

Sliced pitted olives

Chopped onion

1 In a medium bowl, combine all-purpose flour, whole wheat flour, salt and yeast. Add water and stir until combined (the dough will be shaggy and sticky). Cover with plastic wrap and let rise at room temperature for 12 to 24 hours.

2 Preheat the oven to 475°F (240°C).

3 Place dough on a lightly floured work surface. With lightly floured hands, fold dough over onto itself 3 times. Form a ball and cover with plastic wrap. Let stand for 10 minutes.

4 Using a floured rolling pin, roll dough into a 10-inch (25 cm) circle. Place in skillet. Spread pizza sauce evenly over the dough. Sprinkle with toppings (if using).

5 Bake in the preheated oven for 25 to 30 minutes or until crust is crisp and brown, toppings are hot and the cheese is bubbling.

6 Remove skillet from the oven and place on a wire rack. Using a heatproof spatula, transfer pizza from the skillet to a wire rack. Let stand for 10 minutes before cutting.

SAVORY BREADS AND ROLLS

White Bread

Classic white bread is a simple and cherished family staple. This loaf may become your go-to everyday bread, since it's perfect for sandwiches, toast and anytime you just want to enjoy a slice of delicious bread.

Stand mixer

10-inch (25 cm) cast-iron skillet lined with a 15-inch (38 cm) square of parchment paper

3½ cups (875 mL) all-purpose flour (approx.), divided

1 tbsp (15 mL) granulated sugar

2 tsp (10 mL) kosher salt

1½ tsp (7 mL) quick-rising (instant) yeast

1 cup (250 mL) milk

¼ cup (60 mL) water

2 tbsp (30 mL) unsalted butter, thinly sliced

1 large egg, at room temperature

¼ tsp (1 mL) vegetable oil

1 In the bowl of the stand mixer fitted with the paddle attachment, combine 2 cups (500 mL) flour, sugar, salt and yeast.

2 In a microwave-safe glass measuring cup, combine milk, water and butter. Microwave on High until the mixture reaches 120°F to 130°F (49°C to 54°C) and the butter melts, about 45 to 60 seconds.

3 Pour milk mixture into the flour mixture. Beat at medium speed for 1 minute. Add 1 cup (250 mL) flour and the egg. Beat at medium speed for 1 minute. Gradually add remaining ½ cup (125 mL) flour and beat to make a soft dough. If the dough is very sticky, add an additional 2 to 4 tbsp (30 to 60 mL) flour. Replace paddle attachment with the dough hook. Knead until dough is smooth and springs back when pressed lightly with a finger, about 5 minutes.

4 Grease a large bowl with oil. Add dough and turn to coat the top. Cover with a clean dish towel and let rise in a warm, draft-free place for about 1 hour or until doubled in size. Punch down dough and let stand for 10 minutes.

5 Turn dough out onto a lightly floured work surface. Shape into a ball, then pat into an oval about 8 inches (20 cm) long. Place dough in the prepared skillet. Cover with a clean dish towel and let rise in a warm, draft-free place for about 30 to 45 minutes or until doubled in size.

6 Meanwhile, preheat the oven to 350°F (180°C).

7 Using a sharp knife, make 3 slashes in the top of the dough. Bake in the preheated oven for 30 to 35 minutes or until golden brown.

8 Remove skillet from the oven and place on a wire rack. Carefully, using a heatproof spatula, transfer bread to a wire rack. Cool, then slice and serve.

DUTCH OVEN WHITE BREAD

You can bake this classic white bread in a 5-quart (4.7 L) Dutch oven; it will have a crisper and chewier crust. Prepare the bread as directed through Step 4. Then lightly flour a 15-inch (38 cm) square of parchment paper. Shape the dough into a ball and place on the parchment paper. Cover with plastic wrap and let rise for 30 minutes. Meanwhile, place the covered Dutch oven in the oven and preheat to 450°F (230°C). Using a sharp knife, slash an X in the top of the dough. Carefully lift parchment paper with the dough into the hot Dutch oven. Cover with lid and bake for 30 minutes. Uncover and bake for 10 to 15 minutes more, until brown and crisp. Remove Dutch oven and place on a wire rack. Carefully, using a heatproof spatula, transfer the bread to a wire rack. Cool, then slice and serve.

Craft Beer Bread

MAKES 1 LOAF

Craft beers have exploded in popularity in recent years. Lots of small local breweries are creating a huge variety of beers using different hops, malts and yeasts. It's fun to explore all the beers, and equally fun to use them for baking bread. Each beer will flavor the bread just a little differently, but most will taste great. This recipe is easy, so you can make it often.

5-quart (4.7 L) cast-iron Dutch oven with lid

3 cups (750 mL) all-purpose flour (approx.), divided

1½ tsp (7 mL) quick-rising (instant) yeast

1½ tsp (7 mL) kosher salt

1 can or bottle (12 oz/341 mL) beer (see Tips)

2 tbsp (30 mL) unsalted butter, thinly sliced

2 tbsp (30 mL) liquid honey

1 In a large bowl, combine 2 cups (500 mL) flour, yeast and salt.

2 In a microwave-safe glass measuring cup, combine beer and butter. Microwave on High until the mixture reaches 120°F to 130°F (49°C to 54°C) and the butter melts, about 45 to 60 seconds.

3 Pour warm beer mixture and honey into flour mixture. Beat vigorously with a spoon until smooth. Add 1 cup (250 mL) flour, stirring until it forms a thick, sticky batter that pulls away from the sides of the bowl.

4 Cover batter with plastic wrap and let rise at room temperature for 2 hours or until doubled in size.

5 Lightly flour a 15-inch (38 cm) square of parchment paper. Scrape the batter onto the parchment paper and sprinkle with flour. Using floured fingertips, fold the dough over onto itself 2 or 3 times. Shape into a rounded loaf. Cover with plastic wrap and let stand for 30 minutes.

6 Meanwhile, place the covered Dutch oven in the oven and preheat to 450°F (230°C).

7 Carefully lift the parchment paper with the dough into the hot Dutch oven. Cover with lid and bake for 30 minutes. Remove lid and continue to bake for an additional 10 to 15 minutes or until brown and crisp.

8 Remove Dutch oven and place on a wire rack. Carefully, using a heatproof spatula, transfer bread to a wire rack. Cool, then slice and serve.

> **TIPS** | While most beers taste great in this bread, we prefer using a classically flavored lager, IPA or stout and not a sour or fruit-flavored beer. If you choose a light-colored lager, which is a popular beer with a balanced flavor, the bread will have a mild flavor and light color. If you choose to make it with a dark ale or stout, the bread will be darker in color, with a more pronounced beer flavor.
>
> If the beer you choose is not in a 12 oz (341 mL) bottle, measure out the volume you need or add a small amount of water as needed to equal 12 oz (341 mL).

Honey Whole Wheat Bread

MAKES 1 LOAF

With just a touch of honey, this whole wheat bread is ideal to make regularly for your family. Slice and use it for a ham-and-cheese sandwich or have it toasted for breakfast with some butter on top. If you enjoy a softer crust, follow the recipe, but if you like a crisp and chewy crust, follow the tip and bake it in a covered Dutch oven.

Stand mixer

10-inch (25 cm) cast-iron skillet lined with a 15-inch (38 cm) square of parchment paper

2 cups (500 mL) whole wheat flour

2¼ tsp (11 mL) quick-rising (instant) yeast

2 tsp (10 mL) kosher salt

1 cup (250 mL) milk

¼ cup (60 mL) water

2 tbsp (30 mL) unsalted butter, thinly sliced

¼ cup (60 mL) liquid honey

1¼ cups (310 mL) all-purpose flour (approx.), divided

¼ tsp (1 tsp) vegetable oil

1 In the bowl of the stand mixer fitted with the paddle attachment, combine whole wheat flour, yeast and salt.

2 In a microwave-safe glass measuring cup, combine milk, water and butter. Microwave on High until the mixture reaches 120°F to 130°F (49°C to 54°C) and the butter melts, about 45 to 60 seconds.

3 Pour milk mixture and honey into the flour mixture. Beat at medium speed for 1 minute. Add 1 cup (250 mL) all-purpose flour; beat at medium speed for 1 minute. Gradually add remaining ¼ cup (60 mL) all-purpose flour and beat to make a soft dough. If the dough is very sticky, add an additional 2 to 4 tbsp (30 to 60 mL) flour. Replace paddle attachment with the dough hook. Knead until dough is smooth and springs back when pressed lightly with a finger, about 5 minutes.

4 Grease a large bowl with oil. Add dough and turn to coat the top. Cover with a clean dish towel and let rise in a warm, draft-free place for about 1 hour or until doubled in size. Punch down and let stand for 10 minutes.

5 Turn dough out onto a lightly floured work surface. Shape into a ball, then pat into an oval about 8 inches (20 cm) long. Place dough in the prepared skillet. Cover with a clean dish towel and let rise in a warm, draft-free place for about 30 to 45 minutes or until doubled in size.

6 Meanwhile, preheat the oven to 350°F (180°C).

7 Using a sharp knife, make 3 slashes in the top of the dough. Bake in the preheated oven for 30 to 35 minutes or until golden brown.

8 Remove skillet from the oven and place on a wire rack. Using a heatproof spatula, transfer bread to a wire rack. Cool, then slice and serve.

DUTCH OVEN HONEY WHEAT BREAD

If you prefer a crisp and chewy crust, bake this bread in a 5-quart (4.7 L) Dutch oven. Prepare the bread through Step 4. Lightly flour a 15-inch (38 cm) square of parchment paper. Shape dough into a ball and place on the parchment paper. Cover with plastic wrap and let rise for 30 minutes. Meanwhile, place the covered Dutch oven in the oven and preheat to 450°F (230°C). Remove plastic wrap and slash an X in the top of the dough with a sharp knife. Carefully lift parchment paper with the dough into the hot Dutch oven. Put lid on Dutch oven and bake for 30 minutes. Uncover and bake for 10 to 15 minutes more. Remove Dutch oven and place on a wire rack. Carefully, using a heatproof spatula, transfer the bread to a wire rack. Cool, then slice and serve.

Challah Ring

Challah is the traditional bread served on Jewish Shabbat and holidays. This bread is delicious, and while it may look difficult, it's easier than it appears to braid the dough into an elegant ring.

Stand mixer

10-inch (25 cm) cast-iron skillet lined with a 15-inch (38 cm) square of parchment paper

CHALLAH

4½ cups (1.125 L) all-purpose flour (approx.), divided

¼ cup (60 mL) granulated sugar

2¼ tsp (11 mL) quick-rising (instant) yeast

1 tsp (5 mL) salt

1¼ cups (310 mL) warm water (120°F to 130°F/49°C to 54°C)

⅓ cup + ¼ tsp (76 mL) vegetable oil, divided

2 large eggs, at room temperature

1 large egg yolk, at room temperature

TOPPING

1 large egg

1 tbsp (15 mL) water

½ tsp (2 mL) sesame seeds

1 CHALLAH In the bowl of the stand mixer fitted with the paddle attachment, combine 2 cups (500 mL) flour, sugar, yeast and salt. Add warm water, ⅓ cup (75 mL) oil, eggs and egg yolk. Beat on medium-high speed for 1 minute. Stir in 1½ cups (375 mL) flour; beat for 1 minute until combined.

2 Replace paddle attachment with the dough hook. Stir in remaining 1 cup (250 mL) flour to make a soft dough. If dough is very sticky, stir in an additional 2 to 4 tbsp (30 to 60 mL) flour. Knead until dough is smooth and springs back when pressed lightly with a finger, about 5 minutes. Gather dough into a ball.

3 Grease a large bowl with remaining ¼ tsp (1 mL) oil. Add dough and turn to coat the top. Cover with a clean dish towel and let rise in a warm, draft-free place for about 1 hour or until doubled in size. Punch down and let stand for 10 minutes.

4 Turn dough out onto a lightly floured work surface. Divide dough into thirds. Shape each portion into a cylindrical strip about 18 to 20 inches (45 to 50 cm) long. Place the three strips of dough parallel and close together on the work surface. Pinch the top ends of the three strips together. Cross the right strip over the center strip; you now have a new center strip. Cross the left strip over the new center strip. Continue alternating strips until you reach the ends. Pinch the ends together to secure the braid, then shape into a ring.

5 Place dough ring in the skillet. Cover with a clean dish towel and let rise in a warm, draft-free place for 45 to 60 minutes or until doubled in size.

6 Meanwhile, preheat the oven to 350°F (180°C).

7 **TOPPING** In a small bowl, whisk together egg and water. Brush lightly and evenly over the dough, then sprinkle with sesame seeds. Discard remaining egg mixture. Bake in the preheated oven for 40 to 50 minutes or until golden brown. Check the challah during the last 5 to 10 minutes of baking, and cover loosely with foil if browning too quickly.

8 Remove skillet from the oven and place on a wire rack. Using a heatproof spatula, transfer challah to a wire rack. Let cool, then slice and serve.

TIP | If desired, omit the sesame seeds or sprinkle with poppy seeds instead.

Garlic Rolls

We can think of so many meals, such as spaghetti and meatballs and lasagna, that taste better with the addition of garlic rolls. Honestly, great rolls like these involve little effort and make you look like a cooking rock star!

10-inch (25 cm) cast-iron skillet

1 tsp (5 mL) unsalted butter, softened

¼ cup (60 mL) unsalted butter, melted

½ tsp (2 mL) garlic powder

3 garlic cloves, minced

10 frozen white dinner roll yeast dough balls

1 Butter skillet with softened butter.

2 In a small bowl, combine melted butter, garlic powder and minced garlic. Dip each roll into the butter mixture to coat completely. Arrange rolls evenly in the prepared skillet.

3 Loosely cover the skillet with plastic wrap and let dough rise in a warm, draft-free place for 3 to 5 hours or until doubled in size.

4 Preheat the oven to 350°F (180°C).

5 Bake in the preheated oven for 15 to 20 minutes or until golden brown.

6 Remove skillet from the oven and place on a wire rack. Serve rolls warm.

VARIATION

EASY DINNER ROLLS Omit the garlic powder and garlic cloves to make simple and delicious dinner rolls to accompany any meal.

Pull-Apart Herb Rolls

MAKES 8 ROLLS

Soft, fresh, buttery rolls with a hint of herb flavor will add a special touch to any meal.

Stand mixer

10-inch (25 cm) cast-iron skillet

½ cup (125 mL) lukewarm milk (100°F to 115°F/38°C to 46°C)

1¼ tsp (6 mL) quick-rising (instant) yeast

1 tbsp (15 mL) granulated sugar, divided

1 large egg, at room temperature

2 tbsp + 1 tsp (35 mL) unsalted butter, softened and divided

½ tsp (2 mL) salt

1½ cups (375 mL) all-purpose flour (approx.), divided

1 tsp (5 mL) dried parsley

½ tsp (2 mL) dried rosemary, crumbled

½ tsp (2 mL) dried basil

½ tsp (2 mL) garlic powder

¼ tsp (1 mL) vegetable oil

2 tbsp (30 mL) unsalted butter, melted

1 In the bowl of the stand mixer fitted with the paddle attachment, combine lukewarm milk, yeast and 1½ tsp (7 mL) sugar. Cover with plastic wrap and let stand for 5 minutes.

2 Add the remaining sugar, egg, 2 tbsp (30 mL) softened butter, salt, 1 cup (250 mL) flour, parsley, rosemary, basil and garlic powder. Beat at low speed for 30 seconds. Scrape down the sides of the bowl. Add remaining ½ cup (125 mL) flour. Beat at medium speed until dough comes together and pulls away from the sides of the bowl, about 2 minutes.

3 Turn dough out onto a lightly floured work surface and knead for 2 minutes. Grease a medium bowl with oil. Add dough and turn to coat the top. Cover with plastic wrap and let rise for 1 hour or until doubled in size.

4 Grease skillet with the remaining 1 tsp (5 mL) softened butter. Punch down the dough and divide into 8 pieces. Shape each piece into a smooth ball. Arrange evenly in the prepared skillet. Cover with plastic wrap and let rise for 1 hour.

5 Meanwhile, preheat the oven to 350°F (180°C).

6 Bake in the preheated oven for 20 to 25 minutes or until golden brown. Remove skillet from the oven and place on a wire rack. Brush rolls with melted butter. Serve warm or at room temperature.

> TIP | You can use any variety of dried herbs to replace the parsley, rosemary and basil.

Hint of Honey Rolls

MAKES 12 ROLLS

These slightly sweet rolls are an ideal accompaniment for lunch or dinner, and they also make delicious slider-size rolls and cocktail buns. Try slicing a roll in half, then top with mustard and a slice of ham or any of your favorite sandwich fixings. These would be ideal to serve at a tailgate party or whenever friends gather for casual fun.

Stand mixer

10-inch (25 cm) cast-iron skillet

2½ cups (625 mL) all-purpose flour (approx.), divided

2¼ tsp (11 mL) quick-rising (instant) yeast

1 tsp (5 mL) kosher salt

¾ cup (175 mL) buttermilk

3½ tbsp (52 mL) unsalted butter, thinly sliced and divided

3 tbsp (45 mL) liquid honey, divided

1 large egg, at room temperature

1 large egg yolk, at room temperature

¼ tsp (1 mL) vegetable oil

1 tbsp (15 mL) unsalted butter, melted

1 In the bowl of the stand mixer fitted with the paddle attachment, combine 2¼ cups (560 mL) flour, yeast and salt.

2 In a microwave-safe glass measuring cup, combine buttermilk and 3 tbsp (45 mL) butter. Microwave on High until the mixture reaches 120°F to 130°F (49°C to 54°C) and the butter melts, about 45 to 60 seconds.

3 Pour buttermilk mixture into flour mixture. Add 2 tbsp (30 mL) honey, egg and egg yolk. Beat at medium speed for 1 minute. Gradually add remaining ¼ cup (60 mL) flour and beat to make a soft dough. If dough is very sticky, stir in 2 to 4 tbsp (30 to 60 mL) additional flour. Replace paddle attachment with the dough hook. Knead until dough is smooth and springs back when pressed lightly with a finger, about 5 minutes.

4 Grease a large bowl with oil. Add dough and turn to coat the top. Cover with a clean dish towel and let rise in a warm, draft-free place for 1 hour or until doubled in size.

5 Butter the skillet with remaining ½ tbsp (7 mL) butter. Punch down dough and let stand for 10 minutes. Using kitchen scissors, snip the dough into 12 equal pieces. Shape each piece into a smooth ball. Arrange evenly in the prepared skillet. Cover with plastic wrap and let rise for about 30 to 45 minutes or until doubled in size.

6 Preheat the oven to 375°F (190°C).

7 In a small bowl, combine melted butter and remaining 1 tbsp (15 mL) honey. Brush mixture over the rolls.

8 Bake in the preheated oven for 20 to 25 minutes or until golden brown. Check rolls during the last 5 to 10 minutes of baking and cover loosely with foil if browning too quickly.

9 Remove skillet from the oven and place on a wire rack. Serve rolls warm.

Skillet Parker House Rolls

MAKES 11 ROLLS

Kathy's family always includes these old-fashioned rolls as part of their holiday dinner tradition. Named for the Parker House Hotel in Boston, where they were first served, the soft, buttery rolls are experiencing a surge in popularity as more restaurants are serving them again. Best news yet, they are super easy to make with your stand mixer, so no hand kneading is required. The folded rolls are topped with butter at several stages, but we recommend not thinking about it too much and just enjoying the goodness.

Stand mixer

10-inch (25 cm) cast-iron skillet

2½-inch (6 cm) round biscuit cutter or cookie cutter (optional, see page 29)

2½ cups (625 mL) all-purpose flour (approx.)

2 tbsp (30 mL) granulated sugar

2 tsp (10 mL) quick-rising (instant) yeast

¾ tsp (3 mL) kosher salt

⅔ cup (150 mL) milk

2 tbsp (30 mL) unsalted butter, thinly sliced

1 large egg, at room temperature

¼ tsp (1 mL) vegetable oil

¼ cup (60 mL) unsalted butter, melted and divided

1 In the bowl of the stand mixer fitted with the paddle attachment, combine flour, sugar, yeast and salt.

2 In a microwave-safe glass measuring cup, combine milk and butter. Microwave on High until the mixture reaches 120°F to 130°F (49°C to 54°C) and the butter melts, about 30 to 45 seconds.

3 Pour milk mixture into flour mixture; add the egg. Beat at medium speed for 3 minutes, until dough is very soft.

4 Grease a large bowl with oil. Add dough and turn to coat the top. Cover with a clean dish towel and let rise in a warm, draft-free place for 1 hour or until doubled in size. Punch down dough and let stand for 10 minutes.

5 Brush skillet with 1 tbsp (15 mL) melted butter.

6 Turn dough out onto a lightly floured work surface. Using a floured rolling pin, roll into a circle about ½ inch (1 cm) thick. Dust the biscuit cutter with flour and cut rounds of dough. Brush the tops of the rounds with melted butter. Fold each round in half over a table knife to make a crease and pinch edges to seal. Place in the prepared skillet. Reroll the scraps and cut until you have 11 rounds. Brush the top of each roll with melted butter. Cover with plastic wrap and let rise about 30 minutes or until doubled in size.

7 Preheat the oven to 375°F (190°C).

8 Bake in the preheated oven for 18 to 20 minutes or until golden brown.

9 Remove skillet from the oven and place on a wire rack. Brush tops of the baked rolls with remaining melted butter. Serve warm.

Crispy Cast-Iron Skillet Cornbread

MAKES 8 SERVINGS

This classic cornbread is always a hit when we serve it at our cast-iron cooking class. There are a number of different ways to vary the flavor, depending on your taste preference. Coarse stone-ground cornmeal will give more of a corn flavor, while fine cornmeal will give a smoother texture. Also, if you preheat the cast-iron skillet as the recipe directs, the cornbread will develop a crispy golden crust that many people enjoy. But if you prefer a softer cornbread, rub the skillet with the softened butter and pour the batter into a cold pan.

10-inch (25 cm) cast-iron skillet

1 cup (250 mL) coarse-ground yellow cornmeal

1 cup (250 mL) all-purpose flour

6 tbsp (90 mL) granulated sugar

2 tsp (10 mL) baking powder

½ tsp (2 mL) baking soda

½ tsp (2 mL) salt

2 large eggs, at room temperature

¾ cup (175 mL) sour cream

½ cup (125 mL) buttermilk

3 tbsp (45 mL) unsalted butter, melted and cooled slightly

2 tbsp (30 mL) vegetable oil

1 tbsp (15 mL) unsalted butter, softened and thinly sliced

1 Place skillet in the oven and preheat to 425°F (220°C).

2 In a large bowl, whisk together cornmeal, flour, sugar, baking powder, baking soda and salt.

3 In a medium bowl, whisk together eggs, sour cream, buttermilk, melted butter and oil. Pour into cornmeal mixture and stir until combined.

4 Remove skillet from the oven and place on a wire rack. Place softened butter in the skillet. Let stand until the butter is melted. Swirl skillet to evenly coat the pan, then pour in the batter.

5 Bake in the preheated oven for 18 to 20 minutes or until a tester inserted in the center comes out clean.

6 Remove skillet from oven and place on a wire rack. Let cool for 5 minutes. Cut cornbread into squares or wedges and serve warm.

VARIATION

GREEN CHILI CHEESE CORNBREAD Do not preheat the skillet. Stir 1½ cups (375 mL) shredded sharp (old) Cheddar cheese and ½ tsp (2 mL) chili powder into the flour mixture in Step 2. Stir 1 can (4½ oz/127 mL) diced green chiles into the sour cream mixture in Step 3. Pour sour cream mixture into flour mixture. Stir in 1 cup (250 mL) frozen corn, thawed and drained; stir until combined. Rub skillet with the softened butter and pour in the batter. Bake in the preheated oven for 35 to 40 minutes or until a tester inserted in the center comes out clean. Proceed with Step 6.

Bacon Cheese Pinwheels

MAKES 9 ROLLS

These luscious homemade rolls filled with bacon and cheese are perfect to serve with a piping-hot bowl of soup, such as baked potato soup.

Stand mixer

10-inch (25 cm) cast-iron skillet

3 tbsp (45 mL) lukewarm water (100°F to 115°F/38°C to 4°C)

1 tsp (5 mL) quick-rising (instant) yeast

½ tsp (2 mL) granulated sugar

⅓ cup (75 mL) lukewarm milk (100°F to 115°F/38°C to 46°C)

1 large egg, at room temperature

¼ cup (60 mL) unsalted butter, melted and divided

2 cups (500 mL) all-purpose flour (approx.)

1 tsp (5 mL) kosher salt

¼ tsp (1 mL) vegetable oil

4 bacon slices

¼ tsp (1 mL) freshly ground black pepper

1 cup (250 mL) shredded sharp (old) Cheddar cheese

1 In the bowl of the stand mixer fitted with the paddle attachment, combine lukewarm water, yeast and sugar. Let stand for 5 minutes.

2 Add lukewarm milk, egg and 3 tbsp (45 mL) melted butter. Mix on low speed until combined. Add flour and salt and beat for 3 minutes. Turn the dough out onto a lightly floured work surface. Knead until dough is smooth and springs back when pressed with a finger, about 2 minutes.

3 Grease a medium bowl with oil. Add dough and turn to coat the top. Cover with plastic wrap and let rise in a warm, draft-free place for about 1 hour or until doubled in size.

4 Meanwhile, cook bacon in skillet until crisp. Transfer to a plate lined with paper towels to cool, discarding drippings (do not wipe skillet). Crumble bacon.

5 Punch down dough and let stand for 10 minutes. Turn out onto a lightly floured work surface. Using a floured rolling pin, roll dough into a 15- by 9-inch (37.5 by 23 cm) rectangle. Sprinkle bacon evenly over dough and sprinkle with pepper. Sprinkle cheese evenly over the dough. Beginning with a long side, roll the dough, jelly-roll style, into a tight cylinder. Cut into 9 rolls, each about 1½ inches (4 cm) thick.

6 Arrange rolls in the skillet, cut side up, spacing evenly apart. Cover with plastic wrap and let rise in a warm, draft-free place for about 45 minutes or until doubled in size.

7 Meanwhile, preheat the oven to 375°F (190°C).

8 Bake in the preheated oven for 20 to 25 minutes or until golden brown.

9 Remove skillet from the oven and place on a wire rack. Brush hot rolls with remaining 1 tbsp (15 mL) butter. Serve warm.

VARIATION

EXTRA-CHEESY ROLLS Omit the bacon and increase the cheese to 1½ cups (375 mL). Lightly grease skillet with 1 tsp (5 mL) softened butter. Proceed with the recipe as directed.

Cheesy Bacon Onion Skillet Bread

MAKES 8 SERVINGS

This is an ideal accompaniment to any meal but also makes an excellent appetizer to enjoy while watching TV or hosting an informal gathering.

10-inch (25 cm) cast-iron skillet

1 tbsp (15 mL) olive oil

½ cup (125 mL) chopped onion

¼ tsp (1 mL) salt

¼ tsp (1 mL) freshly ground black pepper

1½ cups (375 mL) shredded sharp (old) Cheddar cheese

4 bacon slices, cooked until crisp, crumbled

½ cup (125 mL) unsalted butter, melted

1 can (16.3 oz/462 g) large-size refrigerated biscuits, preferably Southern homestyle or country style

1 Preheat the oven to 375°F (190°C).

2 Heat oil in the skillet over medium-low heat. Add onion and cook, stirring frequently, until soft, about 5 minutes. Remove from the heat. Stir in salt and pepper. Distribute onion evenly in the skillet. Place the skillet on a wire rack. Let cool for 5 minutes.

3 Sprinkle cheese and bacon evenly over the onion.

4 Place melted butter in a small, deep bowl. Cut each biscuit into quarters. Dip each quarter in the butter and place on top of the cheese mixture, arranging evenly in a single layer.

5 Bake in the preheated oven for 20 to 25 minutes or until golden brown.

6 Remove skillet from the oven and place on a wire rack. Let cool for 5 minutes. Wearing oven mitts, carefully invert bread onto a large platter with raised edges. Remove the skillet. Serve warm.

> **TIP** | Substitute Swiss or pepper Jack cheese for the Cheddar cheese, if desired.

SWEET BREADS AND ROLLS

Almond Streusel Bread

MAKES 1 LOAF

We love recipes that look amazing and taste super. This yeast dough bakes into a golden twisted loaf with a crisp crust and a light, tender interior. Hidden inside is a surprising almond streusel filling. Yum!

Stand mixer

Pastry blender (optional)

10-inch (25 cm) cast-iron skillet lined with a 15-inch (38 cm) square of parchment paper

ALMOND BREAD

3¾ cups (925 mL) all-purpose flour (approx.), divided

¼ cup (60 mL) granulated sugar

2¼ tsp (11 mL) quick-rising (instant) yeast

1½ tsp (7 mL) kosher salt

1 cup (250 mL) milk

¼ cup (60 mL) unsalted butter, thinly sliced

½ tsp (2 mL) almond extract

2 large eggs, at room temperature, divided

1 large egg yolk, at room temperature

¼ tsp (1 mL) vegetable oil

1 tbsp (15 mL) water

ALMOND STREUSEL FILLING

½ cup (125 mL) granulated sugar

¼ cup (60 mL) all-purpose flour

¼ tsp (1 mL) ground cinnamon

Pinch salt

¼ tsp (1 mL) almond extract

¼ cup (60 mL) cold unsalted butter, cubed

⅓ cup (75 mL) sliced almonds, toasted and chopped (see page 21)

ALMOND GLAZE

1 cup (250 mL) confectioners' (icing) sugar

1½ tbsp (22 mL) milk

¼ tsp (1 mL) almond extract

1½ tbsp (22 mL) sliced almonds, toasted

1 ALMOND BREAD In the bowl of the stand mixer fitted with the paddle attachment, combine 2 cups (500 mL) flour, sugar, yeast and salt.

2 In a microwave-safe glass measuring cup, combine milk and butter. Microwave on High until the mixture reaches 120°F to 130°F (49°C to 54°C) and butter melts, about 45 to 60 seconds. Add almond extract. Pour milk mixture over flour mixture and beat at medium speed for 2 minutes.

3 Add 1 cup (250 mL) flour, 1 egg and egg yolk. Beat at medium speed for 2 minutes. Gradually add remaining ¾ cup (175 mL) flour and beat to make a soft dough. If the dough is very sticky, stir in an additional 2 to 4 tbsp (30 to 60 mL) flour.

4 Replace paddle attachment with the dough hook. Knead until dough is smooth and springs back when pressed lightly with a finger, about 5 minutes.

continued on page 84

5 Grease a large bowl with oil. Add the dough and turn to coat the top. Cover with a clean dish towel and let rise in a warm, draft-free place for about 1 hour or until doubled in size.

6 ALMOND STREUSEL FILLING
Meanwhile, in a medium bowl, combine sugar, flour, cinnamon, salt and almond extract. Using a pastry blender or two knives, cut in the cold butter until pea-size pieces form. Stir in almonds. Set aside.

7 Punch down dough and let stand for 10 minutes. Turn out onto a lightly floured work surface. Using a floured rolling pin, roll into a 12- by 16-inch (30 by 41 cm) rectangle. Using a sharp knife, cut the dough in half lengthwise to make two 6- by 16-inch (15 by 41 cm) pieces.

8 Spoon half of the streusel filling lengthwise down the center of one dough strip. Fold the dough over lengthwise and seal to make a cylinder about 3 by 16 inches (7.5 by 41 cm). Repeat with the second strip of dough and remaining streusel. Place cylinders parallel on the work surface and pinch at one end to seal the two together. Lift right strip and overlap the left strip. Continue picking up the right strip and overlapping the left, making a rope. Pinch together the ends to secure, then shape into a circle.

9 ALMOND BREAD Place dough circle in the prepared skillet. Cover with a clean dish towel and let rise in a warm, draft-free place for about 45 minutes or until doubled in size. In a small bowl, whisk the remaining egg with the water. Brush the egg mixture over the loaf.

10 Meanwhile, preheat the oven to 350°F (180°C).

11 Bake loaf in the preheated oven for 35 to 45 minutes or until golden brown. Check during the last 10 to 15 minutes of baking, and if browning too quickly, cover loosely with foil.

12 Remove skillet from the oven and place on a wire rack. Using a heatproof spatula, lift bread out of the skillet and place on a wire rack. Let cool completely.

13 ALMOND GLAZE Meanwhile, in a small bowl, whisk together confectioners' sugar, milk and almond extract until smooth. Drizzle glaze over the bread. Garnish with toasted almonds.

Holiday Monkey Bread

MAKES 6 SERVINGS

This recipe has been part of Roxanne's Christmas morning for a long time. She easily puts it together the night before — courtesy of the frozen bread rolls — and then pops it in the oven while the mayhem of unwrapping gifts and checking stockings commences. Traditionally, monkey bread, which is a pull-apart cinnamon bread, is prepared in a Bundt pan and results in leftovers. The beauty of this recipe is that it makes a smaller quantity, which is ideal, since it is best enjoyed the day it is made.

10-inch (25 cm) cast-iron skillet lined with a 15-inch (38 cm) square of parchment paper

Electric mixer

⅓ cup (75 mL) granulated sugar

1½ tsp (7 mL) ground cinnamon, divided

¼ cup (60 mL) unsalted butter, melted

13 frozen white dinner roll yeast dough balls

⅓ cup (75 mL) heavy or whipping (35%) cream

¼ cup (60 mL) packed dark brown sugar

1 In a small bowl, combine granulated sugar and 1 tsp (5 mL) cinnamon. In another small bowl, place melted butter. Dip a dough ball in the butter, then roll in the cinnamon-sugar mixture. Place in the prepared skillet. Continue this process with the remaining 12 frozen rolls, arranging them evenly in the skillet. Using scissors, cut off any overhanging parchment paper. Cover skillet with plastic wrap and refrigerate overnight.

2 Preheat the oven to 325°F (160°C).

3 In a small, deep bowl, using an electric mixer, beat cream at high speed until soft peaks just begin to form. Stir in brown sugar and remaining ½ tsp (2 mL) cinnamon. Dollop cream mixture over each roll and spread evenly.

4 Bake in the preheated oven for 45 to 50 minutes or until golden brown. Remove skillet from the oven and place on a wire rack. Let cool for 10 minutes. Wearing oven mitts, carefully invert bread onto a large platter with raised edges. Remove the skillet. Serve immediately.

> **TIP** | To mix it up, we like to sprinkle the dough with ½ cup (125 mL) coarsely chopped pecans before refrigerating overnight. Proceed with the recipe as directed.

Apple-Butter Rolls with Cider Glaze

MAKES 10 ROLLS

Comforting apple butter, which is seasoned with cinnamon and cloves, reminds many people of a beautiful autumn day. These easy, no-knead rolls are too delicious to serve just during the fall, and since apple butter and apple cider are available all year long, there is no need to wait.

10-inch (25 cm) cast-iron skillet lined with a 15-inch (38 cm) square of parchment paper

APPLE CIDER ROLLS

3 cups (750 mL) all-purpose flour (approx.), divided

¼ cup (60 mL) granulated sugar

2¼ tsp (11 mL) quick-rising (instant) yeast

1 tsp (5 mL) salt

⅔ cup (150 mL) milk

3 tbsp (45 mL) apple cider

¼ cup (60 mL) unsalted butter, thinly sliced

1 large egg, at room temperature

APPLE-BUTTER FILLING

¼ cup (60 mL) apple butter

2 tbsp (30 mL) packed dark brown sugar

1½ tbsp (22 mL) all-purpose flour

¼ tsp (1 mL) ground cinnamon

CIDER GLAZE

1 cup (250 mL) confectioners' (icing) sugar

2 tbsp (30 mL) apple cider

1 APPLE CIDER ROLLS In a large bowl, stir together 2 cups (500 mL) flour, sugar, yeast and salt.

2 In a microwave-safe glass measuring cup, combine milk, cider and butter. Microwave on High until the mixture reaches 120°F to 130°F (49°C to 54°C) and the butter melts, about 45 to 60 seconds. Pour the milk mixture over the flour mixture. Add egg; beat vigorously with a spoon until the mixture is smooth. Stir in an additional 1 cup (250 mL) flour and beat vigorously with a spoon until it forms a soft dough. If the dough is very sticky, stir in an additional 2 to 4 tbsp (30 to 60 mL) flour.

3 Cover the bowl with plastic wrap and let the dough rise in a warm, draft-free place for 20 minutes.

4 Turn dough out onto a lightly floured work surface and shape into a ball. Using a floured rolling pin, roll into a 12-inch (30 cm) square.

5 APPLE-BUTTER FILLING In a small bowl, combine apple butter, brown sugar, flour and cinnamon. Spread the filling lightly over the dough. Beginning with one side, roll the dough, jelly-roll style, into a tight cylinder. Cut into 10 rolls, each about 1¼ inches (3 cm) thick.

6 Arrange rolls in the prepared skillet, cut side up, spacing them about ½ inch (1 cm) apart. Cover with a clean dish towel and let rise in a warm, draft-free place for about 30 to 45 minutes or until doubled in size.

7 Meanwhile, preheat the oven to 375°F (190°C.)

8 Bake rolls in the preheated oven for 30 to 35 minutes or until golden brown. Remove skillet from the oven and place on a wire rack. Let cool for 5 minutes.

9 **CIDER GLAZE** In a small bowl, whisk together confectioners' sugar and cider until smooth. Drizzle the glaze over the rolls. Serve warm.

Eggnog Sweet Rolls

MAKES 10 ROLLS

These rich and inviting rolls are spectacular. With a hint of nutmeg and a splash of rum, they make any morning festive and bring smiles to everyone's face. If your family is like Kathy's, who always have sweet rolls on Christmas morning, these might just become your favorite holiday recipe.

Stand mixer

10-inch (25 cm) cast-iron skillet lined with a 15-inch (38 cm) square of parchment paper

SWEET ROLLS

3 cups (750 mL) all-purpose flour (approx.), divided

3 tbsp (45 mL) granulated sugar

2 tsp (10 mL) quick-rising (instant) yeast

1½ tsp (7 mL) salt

½ tsp (2 mL) ground nutmeg

1 cup (250 mL) eggnog

6 tbsp (90 mL) unsalted butter, thinly sliced

1 large egg, at room temperature

¼ tsp (1 mL) vegetable oil

NUTMEG FILLING

3 tbsp (45 mL) unsalted butter, softened

2 tbsp (30 mL) granulated sugar

1 tsp (5 mL) golden rum (see Tip)

½ tsp (2 mL) vanilla extract

¼ tsp (1 mL) ground nutmeg

EGGNOG FROSTING

1½ cups (375 mL) confectioners' (icing) sugar

2½ tbsp (37 mL) eggnog

1 tbsp (15 mL) golden rum

1 **SWEET ROLLS** In the bowl of the stand mixer fitted with the paddle attachment, combine 1⅓ cups (325 mL) flour, sugar, yeast, salt and nutmeg.

2 In a microwave-safe glass measuring cup, combine eggnog and butter. Microwave on High until the mixture reaches 120°F to 130°F (49°C to 54°C) and the butter melts, about 45 to 60 seconds.

3 Pour eggnog mixture into the flour mixture. Beat at medium speed for 2 minutes. Add 1 cup (250 mL) flour and the egg. Beat at medium speed for 2 minutes. Gradually add remaining ⅔ cup (150 mL) flour and beat to make a soft dough. If the dough is very sticky, add an additional 2 to 4 tbsp (30 to 60 mL) flour. Replace paddle attachment with the dough hook. Knead until the dough is smooth and springs back when pressed lightly with a finger, about 5 minutes.

4 Grease a large bowl with oil. Add dough and turn to coat the top. Cover with a clean dish towel and let rise in a warm, draft-free place for about 1 hour or until doubled in size.

5 Punch down dough and let stand for 10 minutes. Turn dough out onto a lightly floured work surface. Using a floured rolling pin, roll into a 12-inch (30 cm) square.

6 **NUTMEG FILLING** In a small bowl, combine butter, sugar, rum, vanilla and nutmeg; mix until smooth. Spread the mixture evenly over the dough. Beginning with one side, roll the dough, jelly-roll style, into a tight cylinder. Cut into 10 rolls, each about $1\frac{1}{4}$ inches (3 cm) thick.

7 Arrange rolls in the prepared skillet, cut side up, spacing them about $\frac{1}{2}$ inch (1 cm) apart. Cover with a clean dish towel and let rise in a warm, draft-free place for about 30 to 45 minutes or until doubled in size.

8 Meanwhile, preheat the oven to 375°F (190°C.)

9 Bake rolls in the preheated oven for 25 to 35 minutes or until golden brown. Remove skillet from the oven and place on a wire rack. Let cool for 5 minutes.

10 **EGGNOG FROSTING** In a small bowl, whisk together confectioners' sugar, eggnog and rum until smooth. Spread frosting over the rolls. Serve warm.

ALCOHOL-FREE EGGNOG SWEET ROLLS

• • • • • • • • • • • • • • • • • • •

No rum on hand, or avoiding alcohol? Omit the rum in the filling and stir in $\frac{1}{4}$ tsp (1 mL) rum extract instead. Omit the rum in the frosting and increase the eggnog to $3\frac{1}{2}$ tbsp (52 mL).

Pineapple Upside-Down Rolls

MAKES 10 ROLLS

A cast-iron skillet is ideal for caramelizing fruit in classic upside-down desserts. This roll recipe, which is a play on pineapple upside-down cake, really captures that sweet, delicious pineapple flavor. Served warm, these rolls are perfect for brunch.

Stand mixer

10-inch (25 cm) cast-iron skillet

SWEET ROLLS

3 cups (750 mL) all-purpose flour (approx.), divided

3 tbsp (45 mL) granulated sugar

2¼ tsp (11 mL) quick-rising (instant) yeast

1 tsp (5 mL) salt

1 cup (250 mL) milk

¼ cup (60 mL) unsalted butter, thinly sliced

1 large egg, at room temperature

¼ tsp (1 mL) vegetable oil

PINEAPPLE TOPPING

2 cans (each 8 oz/250 g) crushed pineapple, with juice

¼ cup (60 mL) unsalted butter

½ cup (125 mL) packed dark brown sugar

2 tbsp (30 mL) light corn syrup

¼ tsp (1 mL) salt

BROWN SUGAR–GINGER FILLING

2 tbsp (30 mL) unsalted butter, softened

¼ cup (60 mL) packed dark brown sugar

1½ tsp (7 mL) ground ginger

1 SWEET ROLLS In the bowl of the stand mixer fitted with the paddle attachment, combine 1½ cups (375 mL) flour, sugar, yeast and salt.

2 In a microwave-safe glass measuring cup, combine milk and butter. Microwave on High until the mixture reaches 120°F to 130°F (49°C to 54°C) and butter melts, about 45 to 60 seconds.

3 Pour milk mixture into the flour mixture. Beat at medium speed for 2 minutes. Add ½ cup (125 mL) flour and the egg. Beat at medium speed for 2 minutes. Stir in remaining 1 cup (250 mL) flour and beat until it forms a soft dough. If dough is very sticky, stir in an additional ¼ to ½ cup (60 to 125 mL) flour. Replace paddle attachment with the dough hook. Knead until dough is smooth and springs back when pressed lightly with a finger, about 5 minutes.

4 Grease a large bowl with oil. Add dough and turn to coat the top. Cover with a clean dish towel and let rise in a warm, draft-free place for about 1 hour or until doubled in size.

continued on page 92

5 **PINEAPPLE TOPPING** Meanwhile, place pineapple in a fine-mesh sieve set over a bowl. Press pineapple with the back of a spoon to extract the juice. Measure ¾ cup (175 mL) of the juice and pour into the skillet (discard remaining juice). Cook over medium heat, stirring frequently, until reduced by one-third and juice measures ½ cup (125 mL), about 7 minutes. Stir in butter, brown sugar, corn syrup and salt. Cook, stirring frequently, until mixture is hot and sugar dissolves, about 2 minutes.

6 Set aside 2 tbsp (30 mL) crushed pineapple. Stir remaining pineapple into the topping mixture. Set skillet on a wire rack to cool for 15 minutes.

7 Punch down dough and let stand for 10 minutes. Turn out onto a lightly floured work surface. Using a floured rolling pin, roll dough into a 12- by 15-inch (30 by 38 cm) rectangle.

8 **BROWN SUGAR–GINGER FILLING** In a small bowl, stir together reserved 2 tbsp (30 mL) crushed pineapple, softened butter, brown sugar and ground ginger. Spread filling lightly over the dough. Beginning with a long side, roll the dough, jelly-roll style, into a tight cylinder. Cut into 10 rolls, each about 1½ inches (4 cm) thick. Arrange rolls on top of pineapple mixture in skillet, cut side up, spacing them about ½ inch (1 cm) apart. Cover with plastic wrap and let rise in a warm, draft-free place for 15 minutes.

9 Meanwhile, preheat the oven to 375°F (190°C).

10 Bake rolls in the preheated oven for 30 to 35 minutes or until golden.

11 Remove skillet from the oven and place on a wire rack. Let cool for 15 minutes. Gently run a table knife around the edges of the rolls to loosen. Wearing oven mitts, carefully invert rolls onto a large platter with raised edges. Remove the skillet. Serve warm.

Homemade Cinnamon Rolls

MAKES 9 ROLLS

Who doesn't enjoy a great homemade cinnamon roll? It's the perfect combination of crispy outer edges and a warm, gooey center. This recipe hits the mark and you don't even need to use an electric mixer — everything can be prepared in a large bowl.

10-inch (25 cm) cast-iron skillet

CINNAMON ROLLS

1 cup (250 mL) lukewarm milk (100°F to 115°F/38°C to 46°C)

¼ cup (60 mL) vegetable oil

¼ cup (60 mL) granulated sugar

2¼ tsp (11 mL) quick-rising (instant) yeast

2¼ cups (560 mL) all-purpose flour (approx.), divided

¾ tsp (3 mL) salt

¼ tsp (1 mL) baking powder

¼ tsp (1 mL) baking soda

⅓ cup (75 mL) unsalted butter, melted and divided

¾ cup (175 mL) packed dark brown sugar

2 tsp (10 mL) ground cinnamon

ICING

1½ cups (375 mL) confectioners' (icing) sugar

3 tbsp (45 mL) milk

½ tsp (2 mL) vanilla extract

1 CINNAMON ROLLS In a large bowl, combine lukewarm milk, oil, sugar and yeast. Stir in 2 cups (500 mL) flour until combined. Cover with a clean dish towel and let rise in a warm, draft-free place for about 1 hour or until doubled in size.

2 To the bowl, add salt, baking powder, baking soda and remaining ¼ cup (60 mL) flour; stir to form a dough. Turn out onto a lightly floured work surface. Using a floured rolling pin, roll the dough into a 17- by 10-inch (43 by 25 cm) rectangle.

3 Brush 1 tbsp (15 mL) melted butter over the bottom and sides of the skillet. Brush remaining butter over the entire surface of the dough. In a small bowl, combine brown sugar and cinnamon. Sprinkle mixture evenly over the dough. Using your fingertips, lightly pat the sugar mixture into the butter.

4 Beginning with a long side, roll the dough, jelly-roll style, into a tight cylinder. Cut into 9 equal pieces, each about 1¾ inches (4.5 cm) thick. Arrange rolls, cut side up, evenly in the prepared skillet. Cover with a clean dish towel and let rise in a warm, draft-free place for about 40 minutes or until doubled in size.

5 Meanwhile, preheat the oven to 375°F (190°C).

6 Bake rolls in the preheated oven for 18 to 20 minutes or until golden brown. Remove skillet from the oven and place on a wire rack. Let cool for 10 minutes.

7 ICING Meanwhile, in a medium bowl, whisk together confectioners' sugar, milk and vanilla until smooth. Drizzle icing over the rolls. Serve warm or at room temperature.

Maple Pecan Rolls

MAKES 10 ROLLS

Move over, cinnamon rolls. These deliciously sweet rolls, filled with a buttery pecan mixture and topped with a maple syrup glaze, may become your new go-to treat.

Stand mixer

10-inch (25 cm) cast-iron skillet lined with a 15-inch (38 cm) square of parchment paper

SWEET ROLLS

3¼ cups (810 mL) all-purpose flour (approx.), divided

¼ cup (60 mL) granulated sugar

2¼ tsp (11 mL) quick-rising (instant) yeast

1 tsp (5 mL) salt

½ cup (125 mL) water

⅓ cup (75 mL) milk

3 tbsp (45 mL) unsalted butter, thinly sliced

1 large egg, at room temperature

¼ tsp (1 mL) vegetable oil

PECAN FILLING

⅓ cup (75 mL) unsalted butter, melted

¼ cup (60 mL) packed dark brown sugar

1 tsp (5 mL) maple extract

⅔ cup (150 mL) chopped pecans, toasted (see Tip)

MAPLE PECAN GLAZE

¼ cup (60 mL) unsalted butter

¼ cup (60 mL) packed dark brown sugar

3 tbsp (45 mL) pure maple syrup

Pinch salt

3 tbsp (45 mL) milk

⅓ cup (75 mL) chopped pecans, toasted

1 SWEET ROLLS In the bowl of the stand mixer fitted with the paddle attachment, combine 1½ cups (375 mL) flour, sugar, yeast and salt.

2 In a microwave-safe glass measuring cup, combine water, milk and butter. Microwave on High until the mixture reaches 120°F to 130°F (49°C to 54°C) and the butter melts, about 45 to 60 seconds.

3 Pour milk mixture into flour mixture and beat at medium speed for 1 minute. Add 1 cup (250 mL) flour and egg. Beat on medium speed for 2 minutes. Stir in ¾ cup (175 mL) flour. If dough is very sticky, stir in an additional 2 to 4 tbsp (30 to 60 mL) flour. Turn dough out onto a lightly floured work surface and knead for about 5 minutes, until smooth and dough springs back when pressed lightly with a finger.

4 Grease a large bowl with oil. Add dough and turn to coat the top. Cover with a clean dish towel and let rise in a warm, draft-free place for about 1 hour or until doubled in size.

5 Punch down dough and let stand for 10 minutes. Turn out onto a lightly floured work surface. Using a floured rolling pin, roll the dough into a 12-inch (30 cm) square.

continued on page 96

6 **PECAN FILLING** In a small bowl, combine melted butter, brown sugar and maple extract; stir in pecans. Spread filling evenly over dough. Beginning with a long side, roll the dough, jelly-roll style, into a tight cylinder. Cut into 10 rolls, each about 1¼ inches (3 cm) thick.

7 Arrange rolls in the skillet, cut side up, spacing them ½ inch (1 cm) apart. Cover with a clean dish towel and let rise in a warm, draft-free place for about 45 minutes or until doubled in size.

8 Meanwhile, preheat the oven to 375°F (190°C).

9 Bake in the preheated oven for 20 to 25 minutes or until the rolls are golden brown.

10 **MAPLE PECAN GLAZE** Meanwhile, in a small saucepan over medium heat, melt butter. Add brown sugar, maple syrup and salt; whisk until combined. Add milk. Cook, whisking constantly, until mixture comes a boil. Remove from the heat and stir in pecans.

11 Remove skillet from the oven and place on a wire rack. Let cool for 5 minutes. Drizzle glaze over the rolls. Serve warm or let cool to room temperature.

TIP | Toasting the pecans intensifies their flavor. To toast them, spread chopped pecans in a single layer on a rimmed baking sheet. Bake at 350°F (180°C) for 5 to 7 minutes or until lightly browned. Let cool completely, then use as directed.

Giant Skillet Cinnamon Roll

MAKES 1 SKILLET-SIZE ROLL (ABOUT 10 SERVINGS)

This adds a new dimension of fun to traditional cinnamon rolls. Looking for an ideal breakfast after a slumber party? This is guaranteed to produce squeals of delight. Don't strive for perfection when placing the dough strips in the skillet: homestyle and delicious is the goal.

Stand mixer

10-inch (25 cm) cast-iron skillet

CINNAMON ROLL

3 cups (750 mL) all-purpose flour (approx.)

¼ cup (60 mL) granulated sugar

2½ tsp (12 mL) quick-rising (instant) yeast

1 tsp (5 mL) salt

¾ cup + 2 tbsp (205 mL) milk

¼ cup (60 mL) unsalted butter, thinly sliced

2 large eggs, at room temperature

1½ tsp (7 mL) unsalted butter, softened

BROWN SUGAR–CINNAMON FILLING

⅓ cup (75 mL) unsalted butter, softened

½ cup (125 mL) packed dark brown sugar

1 tbsp (15 mL) ground cinnamon

CREAM CHEESE FROSTING

4 oz (125 g) cream cheese, softened

1 cup (250 mL) confectioners' (icing) sugar

2 tbsp (30 mL) unsalted butter, melted

2 tbsp (30 mL) milk

1 CINNAMON ROLL In the bowl of the stand mixer fitted with the paddle attachment, combine flour, sugar, yeast and salt.

2 In a microwave-safe glass measuring cup, combine milk and ¼ cup (60 mL) butter. Microwave on High until the butter melts and the mixture reaches 120°F to 130°F (49°C to 54°C), about 35 seconds.

3 Pour milk mixture into the flour mixture. Add the eggs. Beat until dough pulls away from the sides of the bowl and is soft. If the dough is very sticky, add 2 to 3 tbsp (30 to 45 mL) flour.

4 Turn dough out onto a lightly floured work surface and knead for about 5 minutes, until the dough is smooth and springs back when pressed lightly with a finger. Form into a ball. Cover with a clean dish towel or plastic wrap and let rise in a warm, draft-free place for 30 minutes.

5 Generously grease skillet with the softened butter; set aside.

6 Using a floured rolling pin, roll the dough into a 14- by 12-inch (35 by 30 cm) rectangle.

continued on page 99

7 BROWN SUGAR–CINNAMON FILLING
Spread softened butter all over the dough. In a small bowl, combine brown sugar and cinnamon. Sprinkle mixture evenly over the rectangle. Using your fingertips, lightly pat the sugar mixture into the butter.

8 Cut the dough into 6 equal strips, each about $2\frac{1}{4}$ inches (5.5 cm) wide. Starting with one strip, tightly roll it into a spiral, then wrap an additional strip around it. Place in the center of the prepared skillet. Wrap remaining strips around the dough circle in the skillet. Loosely cover the skillet with plastic wrap and let rise in a warm, draft-free place for $1\frac{1}{2}$ hours or until doubled in size.

9 Meanwhile, preheat the oven to 350°F (180°C).

10 Bake roll in the preheated oven for 30 to 35 minutes or until golden brown. Check during the last 10 to 15 minutes of baking, and if browning too quickly, cover loosely with foil. Remove skillet from the oven and place on a wire rack. Let cool for about 10 minutes.

11 CREAM CHEESE FROSTING
Meanwhile, in the bowl of the stand mixer fitted with the wire whip attachment, beat together cream cheese, confectioners' sugar, butter and milk until smooth. Frost the cinnamon roll. Serve warm.

TIP | For a nutty flavor, sprinkle $\frac{1}{2}$ cup (125 mL) chopped toasted pecans over the cinnamon-sugar mixture at the end of Step 7.

Orange Pecan Rolls

MAKES 8 ROLLS

This recipe provides a little taste of Florida sunshine in each and every bite. You will need approximately three oranges to get the quantity of grated orange zest specified. You can then juice those oranges to use in the recipe.

10-inch (25 cm) cast-iron skillet
Electric mixer

ORANGE ROLLS

⅓ cup (75 mL) milk

1 tsp (5 mL) grated orange zest

⅓ cup (75 mL) orange juice

3 tbsp (45 mL) granulated sugar

2¼ tsp (11 mL) quick-rising (instant) yeast

1 large egg, at room temperature, beaten

1½ tbsp (22 mL) unsalted butter, melted and cooled slightly

½ tsp (2 mL) salt

2⅓ cups (575 mL) all-purpose flour, divided

¼ tsp (1 mL) vegetable oil

1½ tsp (7 mL) unsalted butter, softened

ORANGE FILLING

3 tbsp (45 mL) granulated sugar

1 tsp (5 mL) grated orange zest

3 tbsp (45 mL) unsalted butter, softened

½ cup (125 mL) chopped pecans, toasted (see page 21)

CREAM CHEESE ICING

2 tbsp (30 mL) cream cheese, softened

1 tbsp (15 mL) unsalted butter, softened

¾ cup + 1 tbsp (190 mL) confectioners' (icing) sugar

1 tsp (5 mL) grated orange zest

1 tbsp (15 mL) orange juice

1 ORANGE ROLLS In a microwave-safe glass measuring cup, microwave milk on High until it reaches 100°F to 115°F (38°C to 46°C), about 15 seconds.

2 In a large bowl, combine warm milk, orange zest, orange juice, sugar, yeast, egg, melted butter and salt. Add 1 cup (250 mL) flour; stir to form a lumpy batter. Add remaining 1⅓ cups (325 mL) flour, stirring until a soft dough forms. Cover with a clean dish towel and let rise in a warm, draft-free place for 20 minutes.

3 Turn dough out onto a lightly floured work surface and knead for about 5 minutes, until the dough is smooth and springs back when pressed lightly with a finger.

4 Lightly grease a medium bowl with oil. Add dough and turn to coat the top. Cover with a clean dish towel and let rise in a warm, draft-free place for about a 1½ hours or until doubled in size.

5 Grease the skillet with softened butter. Turn dough out onto a lightly floured work surface. Using a floured rolling pin, roll it into a 12- by 9-inch (30 by 23 cm) rectangle.

6 ORANGE FILLING In a small bowl, combine sugar and orange zest. Spread softened butter evenly over the dough. Sprinkle sugar mixture evenly over the butter. Sprinkle pecans evenly over everything. Beginning with a long side, roll the dough, jelly-roll style, into a tight cylinder. Cut into 8 rolls, each about $1\frac{1}{2}$ inches (4 cm) thick.

7 Arrange rolls in the prepared skillet, cut side up, spacing them evenly apart. Cover with a clean dish towel and let rise in a warm, draft-free place for $1\frac{1}{2}$ hours or until doubled in size.

8 Meanwhile, preheat the oven to 375°F (190°C).

9 Bake rolls in the preheated oven for 15 to 20 minutes or until golden brown. Remove skillet from the oven and place on a wire rack. Let cool for 10 minutes.

10 CREAM CHEESE ICING Meanwhile, in a large bowl, using an electric mixer at medium-high speed, beat together cream cheese, butter, confectioners' sugar, orange zest and orange juice until smooth. Drizzle over slightly warm rolls and spread with a knife to cover them completely.

COFFEE CAKES, COBBLERS AND CRISPS

Peach Almond Coffee Cake

MAKES 10 SERVINGS

Take a moment with friends to enjoy coffee and a slice of this vanilla–sour cream cake filled with peach preserves and topped with a cinnamon-almond streusel. It will be a welcome start to the day.

Electric mixer
Pastry blender (optional)
10-inch (25 cm) cast-iron skillet

CAKE

1½ cups (375 mL) all-purpose flour

½ tsp (2 mL) baking power

½ tsp (2 mL) baking soda

½ tsp (2 mL) salt

½ cup (125 mL) granulated sugar

6 tbsp + 1½ tsp (97 mL) unsalted butter, softened and divided

2 large eggs, at room temperature

¾ cup (175 mL) sour cream

1 tsp (5 mL) vanilla extract

½ cup (125 mL) peach preserves

ALMOND STREUSEL

⅓ cup (75 mL) all-purpose flour

3 tbsp (45 mL) granulated sugar

½ tsp (2 mL) ground cinnamon

3 tbsp (45 mL) cold unsalted butter, cubed

¼ cup (60 mL) sliced almonds, toasted (see page 21)

1 CAKE Preheat the oven to 350°F (180°C).

2 In a medium bowl, whisk together flour, baking powder, baking soda and salt. Set aside.

3 In a large bowl, using an electric mixer at medium-high speed, beat sugar and 6 tbsp (90 mL) butter for 1 minute or until creamy. Add eggs one a time, beating well after each addition. Beat in sour cream and vanilla. Stir in the flour mixture until just combined.

4 ALMOND STREUSEL In a small bowl, combine flour, sugar and cinnamon. Using a pastry blender or two knives, cut in cold butter until pea-size pieces form. Stir in almonds. Set aside.

5 CAKE Grease skillet with the remaining 1½ tsp (7 mL) butter. Spoon half the batter into the prepared skillet and smooth out evenly. Dollop peach preserves over the batter and, using the back of a spoon, gently spread to cover the batter evenly. Top with remaining batter and gently smooth to cover the preserves. Sprinkle evenly with almond streusel.

6 Bake in the preheated oven for 45 to 50 minutes or until a tester inserted in the center comes out clean.

7 Remove skillet from the oven and place on a wire rack. Let cool for 5 minutes. Cut cake into pieces and serve from the skillet.

> **TIP** | Substitute the type of jam or preserves you enjoy most. In addition to peach, our favorites include strawberry and blueberry.

Plum Brunch Cake

MAKES 10 SERVINGS

Sometimes simple flavors are truly the best, which is the case with this coffee cake. The cake is seasoned with a touch of cinnamon and nutmeg, then topped with sliced fresh plums. Brew a pot of coffee or tea and enjoy a slice for brunch or during your morning break.

Electric mixer

10-inch (25 cm) cast-iron skillet

1¼ cups (310 mL) all-purpose flour

½ tsp (2 mL) baking powder

¼ tsp (1 mL) baking soda

¼ tsp (1 mL) salt

½ tsp (2 mL) ground cinnamon, divided

½ tsp (2 mL) ground nutmeg, divided

½ cup + 1 tbsp (140 mL) granulated sugar, divided

½ cup + ½ tbsp (132 mL) unsalted butter, softened and divided

2 tbsp (30 mL) packed dark brown sugar

2 large eggs, at room temperature

¼ cup (60 mL) milk

1 tsp (5 mL) vanilla extract

3 medium purple plums, pitted and sliced about ¾ inch (2 cm) thick

1 tbsp (15 mL) confectioners' (icing) sugar

1 Preheat the oven to 350°F (180°C).

2 In a medium bowl, whisk together flour, baking powder, baking soda, salt, ¼ tsp (1 mL) cinnamon and ¼ tsp (1 mL) nutmeg. Set aside.

3 In a large bowl, using an electric mixer at medium-high speed, beat together ½ cup (125 mL) sugar, ½ cup (125 mL) butter and brown sugar for 2 minutes or until fluffy. Add eggs one a time, beating well after each addition. Beat in milk and vanilla. Stir in flour mixture until just combined.

4 Grease skillet with the remaining ½ tbsp (7 mL) softened butter. Spoon the batter into the prepared skillet and spread evenly. Arrange plums, cut side down, in the batter.

5 In a small bowl, combine remaining 1 tbsp (15 mL) sugar with remaining ¼ tsp (1 mL) cinnamon and ¼ tsp (1 mL) nutmeg. Sprinkle mixture over the plums.

6 Bake in the preheated oven for 35 to 40 minutes or until a tester inserted in the center comes out clean.

7 Remove from the oven and place on a wire rack. Let cool for 5 minutes. Sprinkle with confectioners' sugar. Cut cake into pieces and serve from the skillet.

VARIATION

PEAR BRUNCH CAKE Substitute one sliced pear for the plums. A Bosc pear (cinnamon-colored, with an elongated neck) or a bright green, egg-shaped Anjou pear is a good choice, since they both hold their shape when baked. Peel, core and thinly slice the pear. Proceed with the recipe as directed.

Strawberry Rhubarb Skillet Coffee Cake

MAKES 12 SERVINGS

Strawberries and rhubarb are an undeniable pair. This coffee cake, which features that delicious duo, may become one of your favorites, so go ahead and invite friends to come over and enjoy.

Pastry blender (optional)
10-inch (25 cm) cast-iron skillet
Rimmed baking sheet lined with foil

STRAWBERRY RHUBARB FILLING

4 cups (1 L) frozen, sliced unsweetened strawberries

1½ cups (375 mL) frozen, sliced unsweetened rhubarb

1 tbsp (15 mL) freshly squeezed lemon juice

⅔ cup (150 mL) granulated sugar

3 tbsp (45 mL) cornstarch

CAKE

1½ cups (375 mL) all-purpose flour

½ cup (125 mL) granulated sugar

½ tsp (2 mL) baking powder

½ tsp (2 mL) baking soda

¼ tsp (1 mL) salt

½ cup (125 mL) cold unsalted butter, cubed

¾ cup (175 mL) buttermilk

1 large egg, at room temperature

½ tsp (2 mL) vanilla extract

¼ tsp (1 mL) vegetable oil

TOPPING

⅓ cup (75 mL) all-purpose flour

⅓ cup (75 mL) packed dark brown sugar

3 tbsp (45 mL) unsalted butter, melted

1 Preheat the oven to 350°F (180°C).

2 **STRAWBERRY RHUBARB FILLING** In a large saucepan, combine strawberries, rhubarb and lemon juice. Cook over medium heat for 5 minutes. In a small bowl, combine sugar and cornstarch; stir into fruit mixture. Bring to a boil, stirring constantly, and cook until thickened, about 4 to 5 minutes.

3 **CAKE** In a large bowl, combine flour, sugar, baking powder, baking soda and salt. Using a pastry blender or two knives, cut in cold butter until pea-size pieces form. In a small bowl, whisk together buttermilk, egg and vanilla. Add buttermilk mixture to the flour mixture; stir until no dry flour remains.

4 Grease skillet with oil. Spread half the batter in the skillet and top with the cooked fruit. Drop remaining batter over the fruit by the spoonful.

5 **TOPPING** In a small bowl, combine flour, brown sugar and butter until coarse crumbs form. Evenly sprinkle topping over the batter.

6 Place skillet on the prepared baking sheet. Bake in the preheated oven for 40 to 45 minutes or until top is golden brown and fruit is bubbling.

7 Remove from oven and place on a wire rack. Let cool for 30 minutes. Cut cake into pieces and serve from the skillet.

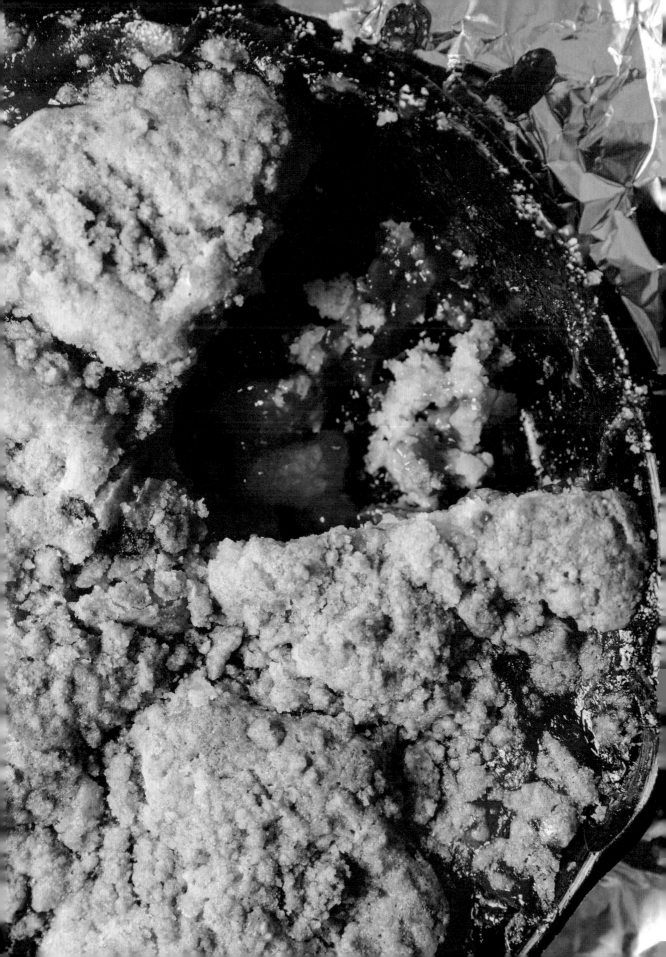

Lemon-Glazed Blueberry Coffee Cake

MAKES 10 SERVINGS

This blueberry-studded coffee cake with its hint of lemon has the fresh look of sunny days. Bake this for yourself or, better yet, give it to a friend or neighbor to brighten their day.

Electric mixer

Pastry blender (optional)

10-inch (25 cm) cast-iron skillet lined with a 15-inch (38 cm) square of parchment paper

COFFEE CAKE

2 cups (500 mL) all-purpose flour

1½ tsp (7 mL) baking powder

½ tsp (2 mL) baking soda

½ tsp (2 mL) salt

1 cup (250 mL) granulated sugar

½ cup (125 mL) unsalted butter, softened

2 large eggs, at room temperature

½ cup (125 mL) milk

1 tsp (5 mL) vanilla extract

2 tsp (10 mL) grated lemon zest

1½ cups (375 mL) fresh or frozen blueberries

STREUSEL TOPPING

½ cup (125 mL) granulated sugar

¼ cup (60 mL) all-purpose flour

¼ cup (60 mL) cold unsalted butter, cubed

½ tsp (2 mL) ground cinnamon

GLAZE

¾ cup (175 mL) confectioners' (icing) sugar

1 tbsp (15 mL) freshly squeezed lemon juice

1 COFFEE CAKE Preheat the oven to 350°F (180°C).

2 In a medium bowl, whisk together flour, baking powder, baking soda and salt. Set aside.

3 In a large bowl, using an electric mixer at medium-high speed, beat together sugar and butter until light and fluffy, about 3 minutes. Add eggs one at a time, beating well after each addition. Beat in milk and vanilla. Stir in lemon zest. Stir in flour mixture until just combined. Gently fold in blueberries. Spread batter evenly in prepared skillet.

4 STREUSEL TOPPING In a small bowl, combine sugar and flour. Using a pastry blender or two knives, cut in cold butter until pea-size pieces form. Stir in cinnamon. Sprinkle evenly over the batter. Bake for 50 to 55 minutes or until a tester inserted in the center comes out clean.

5 Remove skillet from the oven and place on a wire rack. Let cool for 10 minutes. Using the parchment paper, carefully remove the cake and place on a wire rack.

6 GLAZE Meanwhile, in a small bowl, whisk together confectioners' sugar and lemon juice until smooth. Drizzle over cake. Cut cake into pieces and serve warm or at room temperature.

Strawberries and Cream Skillet Cobbler

We both live in the Midwest, where winters can be brutal. On a freezing, below-zero day, we like to prepare this cobbler. Think of a delicious warm version of strawberry shortcake. Treat yourself and enjoy happiness on a cold, gloomy winter day — or perhaps you live in a warmer climate, which can mean rainy, chilly days. Whatever the weather, this is a winner!

10-inch (25 cm) cast-iron skillet

Pastry blender (optional)

1 tsp (5 mL) unsalted butter

5 cups (1.25 L) frozen, sliced unsweetened strawberries

¾ cup (175 mL) granulated sugar

⅓ cup (75 mL) all-purpose flour

1 tbsp (15 mL) freshly squeezed lemon juice

⅛ tsp (0.5 mL) salt

TOPPING

1⅓ cups (325 mL) all-purpose flour (approx.)

1 tbsp (15 mL) baking powder

½ tsp (2 mL) baking soda

½ cup (125 mL) cold unsalted butter, cubed

1 cup + 2 tbsp (280 mL) heavy or whipping (35%) cream, divided

2 tbsp (30 mL) unsalted butter, melted

1½ tbsp (22 mL) coarse white sparkling sugar or turbinado sugar

1 Preheat the oven to 375°F (190°C). Grease skillet with butter.

2 In a large bowl, combine strawberries, sugar, flour, lemon juice and salt. Spoon into the skillet. Some of the flour mixture will remain in the bowl, so use a spoon to sprinkle it evenly over the strawberries in the skillet.

3 **TOPPING** In a large bowl, whisk together flour, baking powder and baking soda. Using a pastry blender or two knives, cut in cold butter until pea-size pieces form. Drizzle ½ cup + 2 tbsp (155 mL) cream over the mixture. Stir to make a soft dough. Using lightly floured hands, form about ⅓ cup (75 mL) dough into a flat biscuit-size round and place on top of the strawberries. Repeat with the remaining dough to make 6 rounds, arranging evenly around the skillet.

4 Brush topping rounds with melted butter and sprinkle evenly with coarse sugar. Bake in the preheated oven for 35 to 40 minutes or until golden brown.

5 Remove skillet from the oven and place on a wire rack. Let cool for 1 hour.

6 Meanwhile, in a small, deep bowl, using an electric mixer at medium-high speed, beat remaining ½ cup (125 mL) cream until stiff. Spoon cobbler into individual serving bowls and top with whipped cream.

Skillet Berry Cobbler

MAKES 12 SERVINGS

This cobbler is guaranteed to elicit oohs and aahs from aro... table. We promise you, the berries combined with the crispy ... create a truly blue-ribbon dessert.

10-inch (25 cm) cast-iron skillet
Rimmed baking sheet lined with foil

10-inch (25 cm) Double Pie Crust
(page 151), prepared through Step 3,
or two 9-inch (23 cm) store-bought pie
crusts, rolled out (see Tip)

5 cups (1.25 L) frozen unsweetened mixed
berries (about two 12-oz/375 g packages)

¼ cup (60 mL) unsalted butter, melted

1 tsp (5 mL) freshly squeezed lemon juice

1¼ cups (310 mL) granulated sugar,
divided

½ cup (125 mL) all-purpose flour

½ cup (125 mL) water

¼ cup (60 mL) unsalted butter, cubed

Vanilla ice cream (optional)

1 Preheat the oven to 375°F (190°C).

2 Pierce bottom and sides of the prepared crust with the tines of a fork. Bake in the preheated oven for 9 minutes. Set aside.

3 In a large bowl, combine frozen berries, butter, lemon juice, 1 cup (250 mL) sugar and flour. Gently spoon mixture into the pie crust. Some of the mixture will be left in the bowl, so use a spoon to sprinkle it evenly over the berries. Drizzle with water.

4 Unfold the second pie crust and place over the berries (the edges of a cobbler crust are not fluted). Using a knife, cut five slits in the crust. Scatter butter over the crust and sprinkle evenly with remaining ¼ cup (60 mL) sugar. Place skillet on the prepared baking sheet. Bake in the preheated oven for 1 hour and 15 minutes to 1 hour and 25 minutes, or until top crust is crisp and berry mixture is bubbling.

5 Remove skillet from the oven and place on a wire rack. Let cool for 30 minutes. Serve warm with vanilla ice cream on the side (if using).

> TIP | In a hurry? You can substitute 2 store-bought refrigerated 9-inch (23 cm) pie crusts for the homemade. Let the pastry come to room temperature and unroll according to the package directions. Roll out each crust to make it thinner, approximately 10 inches (25 cm) in diameter. Proceed with recipe as directed.

Cherry Cobbler

MAKES 12 SERVINGS

Here's a quick cherry primer to guarantee success: There's a difference between sweet cherries, such as Bing, and tart cherries. Sweet, dark cherries are great for eating fresh from your hand, while tart cherries are slightly smaller and usually bright red in color. This recipe calls for frozen tart cherries (don't thaw the cherries; use them frozen). Perfect to serve with a dollop of vanilla ice cream on top.

10-inch (25 cm) cast-iron skillet
Rimmed baking sheet lined with foil

5 cups (1.25 L) frozen pitted tart cherries (about two 12-oz/375 g packages)

1½ cups (375 mL) granulated sugar

½ cup + ⅓ cup (200 mL) water, divided

¼ cup (60 mL) cornstarch

1 tsp (5 mL) almond extract

1 tsp (5 mL) unsalted butter

All-purpose flour

10-inch (25 cm) Single Deep-Dish Pie Crust (page 150), prepared through Step 2

Vanilla ice cream (optional)

1 Preheat the oven to 375°F (190°C).

2 In a medium saucepan over medium-high heat, combine cherries, sugar and ½ cup (125 mL) water. Bring mixture to a boil, stirring frequently.

3 In a small bowl, combine remaining ⅓ cup (75 mL) water and cornstarch until smooth. Stir into cherry mixture. Bring to a boil, stirring constantly, and cook until mixture thickens. Remove from heat and stir in almond extract.

4 Grease skillet on the bottom and sides with butter. Pour cherry mixture into the skillet.

5 On a lightly floured work surface, using a floured rolling pin, roll out the pie crust into a 12-inch (30 cm) circle. Cut into six 2-inch (5 cm) strips. Arrange three strips on top of the cherries, spacing them evenly. Fold the center one back until it almost falls out of the skillet. Place a strip near the end where it's still attached, close to the edge of the pan and perpendicular to the original strips. Fold the center strip down across the newly placed strip. Fold the two original outside strips back to where they are held down by the new strip. Place another strip in the center of the pie, perpendicular to the original strips. Fold the two original outside strips back down. Repeat with the last strip, placing it near the other side of the pan so that it lies on top of the original outside strips and underneath the center strip. It will look like a lattice pattern. Trim off any excess and seal the ends to the edges of the skillet. The look will be rustic – it does not need to be perfect.

6 Place skillet on the prepared baking sheet. Bake in the preheated oven for 55 to 65 minutes or until crust is brown and cherries are bubbling.

7 Remove skillet from the oven and place on a wire rack. Let cool for 1 hour. Spoon cobbler into individual serving bowls and top with vanilla ice cream (if using).

Peach Cobbler with Brown-Sugar Biscuit Top

MAKES 8 SERVINGS

There just can't be a summer without peach cobbler — at le
Kathy's house. This delicious version features brown-sugar biscuits, so
the flavor is comforting and inviting. Top your serving with sweetened
whipped cream.

10-inch (25 cm) cast-iron skillet
Pastry blender (optional)
Electric mixer

¼ tsp (1 mL) vegetable oil

5 cups (1.25 L) peeled, pitted, sliced peaches (about 7 medium; see Tips)

1 tbsp (15 mL) freshly squeezed lemon juice

¼ cup (60 mL) granulated sugar

¼ cup (60 mL) packed brown sugar

2 tbsp (30 mL) all-purpose flour

BROWN-SUGAR BISCUIT TOPPING

1½ cups (375 mL) all-purpose flour

¼ cup (60 mL) packed brown sugar

2½ tsp (12 mL) baking powder

½ tsp (2 mL) salt

6 tbsp (90 mL) cold unsalted butter, cubed

1¾ cups (425 mL) heavy or whipping (35%) cream, divided

2 tbsp (30 mL) confectioner's (icing) sugar

1 Preheat the oven to 400°F (200°C).

2 Grease skillet with oil. Put peaches in the skillet and drizzle with lemon juice. In a small bowl, whisk together granulated sugar, brown sugar and flour. Sprinkle mixture over peaches.

3 BROWN-SUGAR BISCUIT TOPPING In a large bowl, combine flour, brown sugar, baking powder and salt. Using a pastry blender or two knives, cut in cold butter until pea-size pieces form. Add ¾ cup (175 mL) cream and stir until moistened and no dry flour remains. Dollop the batter by tablespoonfuls over the peaches.

4 Bake in the preheated oven for 50 to 60 minutes or until biscuits are golden brown and filling is bubbling.

5 Remove skillet from the oven and place on a wire rack. Let cool for 15 minutes.

6 Meanwhile, in a small, deep bowl, using an electric mixer at medium-high speed, beat remaining 1 cup (250 mL) cream with confectioners' sugar until stiff peaks form. Spoon cobbler into individual serving bowls and top with whipped cream.

> TIPS | You can substitute 5 cups (1.25 L) frozen, sliced unsweetened peaches (about one and a half 16-oz/500 g packages) for the fresh, if desired.
>
> Omit the whipped cream and top with cinnamon or vanilla ice cream, if desired.

Caramel Apple Pecan Crisp

MAKES 10 SERVINGS

Sweet and buttery caramel dripping down the sides of a tart apple is the perfect combination of flavors. You can capture them in this apple crisp dessert. It just can't get any better — or maybe it can, if you top it with a scoop of ice cream and an extra drizzle of caramel sauce.

10-inch (25 cm) cast-iron skillet

Pastry blender (optional)

1 tsp (5 mL) unsalted butter, softened

6 cups (1.5 L) peeled and thinly sliced Granny Smith apples (about 5 apples or 2¼ lbs/1.125 kg)

1 tbsp (15 mL) freshly squeezed lemon juice

½ cup (125 mL) caramel topping (see Tip)

TOPPING

¾ cup (175 mL) all-purpose flour

¾ cup (175 mL) large-flake (old-fashioned) rolled oats

¼ cup (60 mL) packed dark brown sugar

1 tsp (5 mL) ground cinnamon

¼ tsp (1 mL) salt

6 tbsp (90 mL) cold unsalted butter, cubed

½ cup (125 mL) chopped toasted pecans (see page 21)

Vanilla or cinnamon ice cream (optional)

Caramel topping (optional)

1 Preheat the oven to 350°F (180°C).

2 Grease skillet with butter. Put the apples in the skillet. Drizzle with lemon juice and caramel topping.

3 **TOPPING** In a medium bowl, combine flour, oats, brown sugar, cinnamon and salt. Using a pastry blender or two knives, cut in cold butter until pea-size pieces form. Stir in pecans. Sprinkle topping evenly over the apples.

4 Bake in the preheated oven for 50 to 60 minutes or until topping is golden brown and apples are tender.

5 Remove skillet from the oven and place on a wire rack. Let cool for 15 minutes. Spoon the crisp into individual serving bowls and top with vanilla ice cream and caramel topping (if using).

> TIP | What's the difference between caramel topping and caramel sauce? While similar in flavor, the topping is thicker — so thick that you may need to spoon it out of the jar. While either can be used in this recipe, we think thicker is better for this recipe.

Blackberry Crumble

MAKES 8 SERVINGS

Juicy blackberries, sweetened and simmered underneath a buttery crumble topping, make the best dessert. Quick and simple to assemble, this is an ideal dessert for any night of the week.

10-inch (25 cm) cast-iron skillet

Pastry blender (optional)

1 tsp (5 mL) unsalted butter, softened

5 cups (1.25 L) frozen unsweetened blackberries (about one and a half 16-oz/500 g packages)

1 tbsp (15 mL) freshly squeezed lemon juice

⅔ cup (150 mL) granulated sugar

2 tbsp (30 mL) cornstarch

TOPPING

1 cup (250 mL) all-purpose flour

⅔ cup (150 mL) packed dark brown sugar

1 tsp (5 mL) ground cinnamon

¼ tsp (1 mL) salt

½ cup (125 mL) cold unsalted butter, cubed

Vanilla ice cream (optional)

1 Preheat the oven to 375°F (190°C).

2 Grease skillet with butter. Place blackberries in the skillet and drizzle with lemon juice. In a small bowl, whisk together sugar and cornstarch. Sprinkle mixture over the berries.

3 **TOPPING** In a medium bowl, combine flour, brown sugar, cinnamon and salt. Using a pastry blender or two knives, cut in cold butter until pea-size pieces form. Using your fingertips, mash the mixture together to form large clumps. Sprinkle mixture evenly over the berries.

4 Bake in the preheated oven for 40 to 45 minutes or until topping is golden brown and the filling is bubbling.

5 Remove skillet from the oven and place on a wire rack. Let cool for 15 minutes. Spoon the crumble into individual serving bowls and top with vanilla ice cream (if using).

BISCUITS AND SCONES

Buttery Skillet Biscuits

MAKES 8 BISCUITS

If you like a crispy, crunchy biscuit with a soft, tender interior, then these are for you. This recipe uses pantry staples to produce a warm, satisfying biscuit that will make any breakfast exceptional. You can easily pull the biscuits together if you've got a bit of extra time in the morning.

Pastry blender (optional)
10-inch (25 cm) cast-iron skillet
2¼-inch (5.5 cm) ice-cream scoop
(optional)

2 cups (500 mL) all-purpose flour

1 tbsp (15 mL) baking powder

1 tsp (5 mL) salt

¼ tsp (1 mL) baking soda

½ cup (125 mL) cold unsalted butter, cubed

¾ cup (175 mL) milk (approx.)

2 tbsp (30 mL) unsalted butter, melted

1 Preheat the oven to 450°F (230°C).

2 In a large bowl, combine flour, baking powder, salt and baking soda. Using a pastry blender or two knives, cut in cold butter until pea-size pieces form.

3 Add ¾ cup (175 mL) milk to the bowl and mix until the flour is moistened and no dry flour remains. You may need to add up to ¼ cup (60 mL) more milk. The dough will be lumpy — do not overmix.

4 Drop ¼-cup (60 mL) mounds of dough into the skillet, using a 2¼-inch (5.5 cm) ice-cream scoop, if you have one. Brush tops of the mounds with melted butter. Bake in the preheated oven for 18 to 21 minutes or until golden brown.

5 Remove skillet from the oven and place on a wire rack. Using a heatproof spatula, transfer the biscuits to the wire rack and let cool for 5 minutes. Serve warm.

VARIATION

BUTTERY BACON BISCUITS After the cold butter has been cut in at the end of Step 2, add 3 strips of bacon, cooked and crumbled, to the mixture. Proceed with the recipe as directed.

Yeast-Raised Angel Biscuits

When you crave something that is a cross between a traditional biscuit and a dinner roll, this recipe is the ticket. These delicious biscuits are light and fluffy, with a hint of yeast flavor. We like to enjoy these on mornings when we're not in a hurry, to allow for the 1-hour rising time.

Pastry blender (optional)

10-inch (25 cm) cast-iron skillet

2¹⁄₂-inch (6 cm) round biscuit or cookie cutter (optional, see page 29)

¼ cup (60 mL) lukewarm water (100°F to 115°F/38°C to 46°C)

¼ cup + 1 tsp (65 mL) granulated sugar, divided

2¼ tsp (11 mL) quick-rising (instant) yeast

2½ cups (625 mL) all-purpose flour (approx.)

1¼ tsp (6 mL) baking powder

1 tsp (5 mL) salt

½ tsp (2 mL) baking soda

¼ cup (60 mL) cold unsalted butter, cubed

¼ cup (60 mL) shortening

1 cup (250 mL) buttermilk (see page 20)

2 tbsp (30 mL) unsalted butter, melted

1 In a small bowl, combine lukewarm water, 1 tsp (5 mL) sugar and yeast. Set aside.

2 In a large bowl, whisk together remaining ¼ cup (60 mL) sugar, flour, baking powder, salt and baking soda. Using a pastry blender or two knives, cut in cold butter and shortening until pea-size pieces form.

3 Add the yeast mixture and buttermilk to the flour mixture; stir until combined and a dough forms. Turn dough onto a lightly floured surface and gently knead until you have a soft dough.

4 Fold dough onto itself 5 times. Pat into a circle 1 inch (2.5 cm) thick. Dust the biscuit cutter with flour and cut rounds of dough. Place rounds in skillet. Gather together scraps of dough, pat until 1 inch (2.5 cm) thick, and continue to cut until you have 10 rounds in the skillet. Cover skillet with plastic wrap and let rise in a warm, draft-free place for 1 hour.

5 Preheat the oven to 400°F (200°C).

6 Brush tops of dough rounds with melted butter. Bake in the preheated oven for 15 to 18 minutes or until lightly browned.

7 Remove skillet from the oven and place on a wire rack. Using a heatproof spatula, serve biscuits warm from the skillet.

> TIPS | If desired, brush the baked biscuits with an additional 2 tbsp (30 mL) melted butter before serving.

Cheddar Chive Biscuits

MAKES 8 BISCUITS

Jewels of Cheddar cheese and chives stud these moist yet crisp bis
This is a perfect accompaniment to so many meals, such as
stew and braised meat. However, these biscuits are equally delish as
a breakfast sandwich, filled with crisp bacon, a cooked sausage patty
or a slice of ham.

Pastry blender (optional)

*3-inch (7.5 cm) round biscuit cutter
or cookie cutter (optional, see
page 29)*

10-inch (25 cm) cast-iron skillet

2 cups (500 mL) all-purpose flour
(approx.)

2 tsp (10 mL) baking powder

1 tsp (5 mL) granulated sugar

½ tsp (2 mL) baking soda

½ tsp (2 mL) salt

¾ cup (175 mL) shredded sharp (old)
Cheddar cheese

¼ cup (60 mL) minced fresh chives

6 tbsp (90 mL) cold unsalted butter,
cubed

¾ cup (175 mL) buttermilk (approx.)

2 tbsp (30 mL) unsalted butter, melted

1 Preheat the oven to 425°F (220°C).

2 In a large bowl, combine flour, baking
powder, sugar, baking soda and salt.
Add Cheddar cheese and chives; stir to
combine. Using a pastry blender or two
knives, cut in cold butter until pea-size
pieces form.

3 Add ¾ cup (175 mL) buttermilk to bowl
and stir until flour is moistened and no
dry flour remains. You may need to add
up to ¼ cup (60 mL) more buttermilk.
With lightly floured hands, gather dough
into a ball in the bowl. Transfer dough
to a lightly floured surface and knead 5
or 6 times. Pat into a circle about ¾ inch
(2 cm) thick. Dust the biscuit cutter with
flour and cut rounds of dough. Place
in skillet. Gather together scraps of
dough, pat until ¾ inch (2 cm) thick, and
continue to cut until you have 8 rounds in
skillet.

4 Brush tops of dough rounds with
melted butter. Bake in the preheated
oven for 16 to 18 minutes or until
golden brown.

5 Remove skillet from the oven and
place on a wire rack. Using a heatproof
spatula, transfer biscuits to a wire rack
and let cool for 5 minutes. Serve warm.

> **TIP** | For traditional buttermilk
> biscuits, omit the cheese and chives
> and continue with the recipe as
> directed.

Maple Bacon Biscuits

MAKES 7 BISCUITS

Maple and bacon are two iconic flavors that just seem to go together, and these biscuits capture that sweet and salty magic. This makes them delicious for breakfast and equally as delicious as an accompaniment for lunch or dinner. Serve with just a smear of butter or split and top with apple butter or Cheddar cheese for a quick sandwich or appetizer.

Pastry blender (optional)

2¹/₂-inch (6 cm) round biscuit or cookie cutter (optional, see page 29)

10-inch (25 cm) cast-iron skillet

1¾ cups (425 mL) all-purpose flour (approx.)

1 tbsp (15 mL) granulated sugar

2 tsp (10 mL) baking powder

½ tsp (2 mL) baking soda

½ tsp (2 mL) salt

6 tbsp (90 mL) cold unsalted butter, cubed

8 oz (250 g) bacon, cooked and crumbled

⅓ cup (75 mL) buttermilk, approx. (see page 20)

¼ cup (60 mL) pure maple syrup, divided

1 large egg, at room temperature

1 Preheat the oven to 400°F (200°C).

2 In a large bowl, whisk together flour, sugar, baking powder, baking soda and salt. Using a pastry blender or two knives, cut in cold butter until pea-size pieces form. Stir in bacon.

3 In a small bowl, whisk together buttermilk, 3 tbsp (45 mL) maple syrup and egg. Pour over the flour mixture and stir until lightly moistened. You may need to add up to 2 tbsp (30 mL) more buttermilk. With lightly floured hands, gather dough into a ball in the bowl. Turn the dough out onto a lightly floured surface and knead 5 or 6 times. Pat into a circle about ¾ inch (2 cm) thick. Dust the biscuit cutter with flour and cut rounds of dough. Place in skillet. Gather together scraps of dough, pat until ¾ inch (2 cm) thick, and continue to cut until you have 7 rounds in the skillet.

4 Bake in the preheated oven for 15 minutes or until biscuits are set and just beginning to brown. Brush top of biscuits with remaining 1 tbsp (15 mL) maple syrup. Bake for 4 to 6 minutes more or until lightly browned.

5 Remove skillet from the oven and place on a wire rack. Using a heatproof spatula, transfer biscuits to a wire rack and let cool for 5 minutes. Serve warm.

Cinnamon Raisin Biscuits

MAKES 7 BISCUITS

If you are often tempted to stop by a local diner or fast-food restaurant to buy a treat to go with your coffee, then you will especially enjoy this recipe. These slightly sweet biscuits are chock-full of raisins and then finished with a vanilla glaze. They're sweet, but not too sweet, so adults and children alike will enjoy these comforting treats.

Pastry blender (optional)

2¹/₂-inch (6 cm) round biscuit cutter or cookie cutter (optional, see page 29)

10-inch (25 cm) cast-iron skillet

BISCUITS

1 cup (250 mL) boiling water

½ cup (125 mL) dark raisins (see Tip)

1¾ cups (425 mL) all-purpose flour (approx.)

2½ tbsp (37 mL) granulated sugar

2 tsp (10 mL) baking powder

1 tsp (5 mL) ground cinnamon

½ tsp (2 mL) salt

6 tbsp (90 mL) cold unsalted butter, cubed

⅔ cup (150 mL) milk (approx.)

1 tbsp (15 mL) unsalted butter, melted

VANILLA GLAZE

¾ cup (175 mL) confectioners' (icing) sugar

1½ tbsp (22 mL) milk

½ tsp (2 mL) vanilla extract

1 BISCUITS In a small bowl, pour boiling water over raisins. Let stand for 15 minutes. Drain.

2 Preheat the oven to 425°F (220°C).

3 In a large bowl, combine flour, sugar, baking powder, cinnamon and salt. Using a pastry blender or two knives, cut in cold butter until pea-size pieces form. Stir in raisins. Add milk to bowl and stir until flour is moistened and no dry flour remains. You may need to add up to ¼ cup (60 mL) more milk. With lightly floured hands, gather dough into a ball in the bowl. Transfer dough to a lightly floured surface and knead 5 or 6 times. Pat into a circle about 1 inch (2.5 cm) thick. Dust the biscuit cutter with flour and cut rounds of dough. Place in skillet. Gather together scraps of dough, pat until 1 inch (2.5 cm) thick, and continue to cut until you have 7 rounds in the skillet.

4 Brush tops of dough rounds with the melted butter. Bake in the preheated oven for 18 to 20 minutes or until golden brown.

5 Remove skillet from the oven and place on a wire rack. Using a heatproof spatula, transfer biscuits to a wire rack and let cool for 5 minutes.

6 VANILLA GLAZE Meanwhile, in a small bowl, whisk together confectioners' sugar, milk and vanilla until smooth. Spread glaze over each biscuit. Serve warm.

TIP | If desired, substitute sweetened dried cranberries for the raisins.

Cream Tea Scones

MAKES 8 SCONES

Ever since we traveled to London on a business trip and happened upon afternoon tea at the lovely Dorchester Hotel, we have been obsessed with scones and afternoon tea. Back home we teach cooking classes at a local gourmet food shop, and we often offer a tea class complete with scones, tea sandwiches and sweet treats. This recipe always gets rave reviews from our students. Cream tea scones are best enjoyed the day they are baked, but if that isn't possible, they freeze nicely for up to 2 months. We love serving these with clotted cream and jam.

10-inch (25 cm) cast-iron skillet

2 cups (500 mL) all-purpose flour (approx.)

⅓ cup (75 mL) granulated sugar

1 tbsp (15 mL) baking powder

½ tsp (2 mL) salt

1 tsp (5 mL) vanilla extract

1¼ cups + 1 tbsp (325 mL) heavy or whipping (35%) cream, divided

1½ tbsp (22 mL) coarse white sparkling sugar or turbinado sugar

1 Preheat the oven to 425°F (220°C).

2 In a large bowl, whisk together flour, sugar, baking powder and salt. Pour vanilla over flour mixture.

3 Drizzle 1¼ cups (310 mL) cream over the flour mixture. Stir gently until a dough forms. With lightly floured hands, gather dough into a ball in the bowl. Transfer dough to a lightly floured surface. Using both hands, pat into a 7-inch (18 cm) disk about ¾ to 1 inch (2 to 2.5 cm) thick. Cut disk in half and cut each half into 4 to yield 8 wedges. Brush wedges with remaining 1 tbsp (15 mL) cream. Sprinkle with coarse sugar. Place wedges in a circle in skillet.

4 Bake in the preheated oven for 18 to 20 minutes or until scones are starting to brown and spring back when gently poked with a finger.

5 Remove skillet from the oven and place on a wire rack. Using a heatproof spatula, transfer scones to a wire rack and let cool for 5 minutes. Serve warm.

VARIATION

CHOCOLATE CHIP SCONES Prepare scones through Step 2. Stir in ¾ cup (175 mL) mini semisweet chocolate chips. Proceed with the recipe as directed.

Rum Raisin Scones

MAKES 8 SCONES

Invite friends for tea and serve these memorable scones. Th[...]
quite subtle and will have your friends asking, "What is that [...]
flavor in here?"

Pastry blender (optional)
10-inch (25 cm) cast-iron skillet

⅔ cup (150 mL) dark raisins

⅔ cup (150 mL) golden rum (see Tip)

2¼ cups (560 mL) all-purpose flour (approx.)

⅓ cup (75 mL) granulated sugar

2 tsp (10 mL) baking powder

1 tsp (5 mL) baking soda

½ tsp (2 mL) salt

6 tbsp (90 mL) cold unsalted butter, cubed

¾ cup (175 mL) sour cream

1 large egg, at room temperature

1 In a small bowl, combine raisins and rum. Let stand at room temperature for at least 1 hour or up to 2 hours. (Or cover and refrigerate overnight; let come to room temperature before baking.)

2 Preheat the oven to 425°F (220°C).

3 In a large bowl, whisk together flour, sugar, baking powder, baking soda and salt. Using a pastry blender or two knives, cut in cold butter until pea-size pieces form. Drain raisins, reserving rum. Stir raisins into the flour mixture.

4 In a small bowl, whisk together sour cream, egg and ⅓ cup (75 mL) reserved rum. Pour over the flour mixture and stir gently to make a soft dough. You may need to add up to 1 tbsp (15 mL) more reserved rum (discard any remaining rum). With lightly floured hands, gather dough into a ball in the bowl. Transfer dough to a lightly floured surface. Using both hands, pat into a 9-inch (23 cm) disk about ¾ inch (2 cm) thick. Cut disk in half and cut each half into 4 to yield 8 wedges. Gently lift wedges with a spatula and place in a circle in the skillet.

5 Bake in the preheated oven for 20 to 25 minutes or until golden brown.

6 Remove skillet from the oven and place on a wire rack. Let cool for 5 minutes. If needed, use a sharp knife to cut the wedges apart. Using a heatproof spatula, transfer scones to a wire rack and let cool for 5 minutes. Serve warm.

> TIP | If you prefer, substitute an equal amount of water flavored with ½ tsp (2 mL) rum extract for the rum.

Buttermilk Blueberry Scones

MAKES 8 SCONES

This scone recipe has become a family favorite. Roxanne's daughter is not a big fan of scones, but when she tasted this version filled with blueberries, she crossed over and gave it a five-star rating, exclaiming, "It's more like a blueberry muffin scone, and I love it!" It does combine the best of both and is sure to be earmarked in your book, too.

Pastry blender (optional)
10-inch (25 cm) cast-iron skillet

2 cups (500 mL) all-purpose flour (approx.)

¼ cup (60 mL) granulated sugar

¼ cup (60 mL) packed dark brown sugar

1 tbsp (15 mL) baking powder

½ tsp (2 mL) salt

½ tsp (2 mL) ground cinnamon

½ cup (125 mL) cold unsalted butter, cubed

1 cup (250 mL) fresh or frozen blueberries

⅔ cup (150 mL) buttermilk (see page 20)

2 large eggs, at room temperature and divided

1 tsp (5 mL) vanilla extract

1½ tbsp (22 mL) coarse white sparkling sugar or turbinado sugar

1 Preheat the oven to 400°F (200°C).

2 In a large bowl, whisk together flour, granulated sugar, brown sugar, baking powder, salt and cinnamon. Using a pastry blender or two knives, cut in cold butter until pea-size crumbs form. Gently stir in blueberries.

3 In a medium bowl, whisk together buttermilk, 1 egg and vanilla. Add to the flour mixture and stir until the flour is moistened and no dry flour remains. With lightly floured hands, gather dough into a ball in the bowl. Transfer dough to a lightly floured surface. Form into an 8-inch (20 cm) disk about ¾ inch (2 cm) thick. Cut disk in half and cut each half into 4 to yield 8 wedges. Carefully, using a spatula, move wedges to the skillet, placing in a circle.

4 In a small bowl, whisk remaining egg. Brush tops of wedges with egg, then sprinkle evenly with coarse sugar.

5 Bake in the preheated oven for 22 to 25 minutes or until golden brown. Remove skillet from the oven and place on a wire rack. If needed, use a sharp knife to cut wedges apart. Using a heatproof spatula, transfer scones to a wire rack and let cool for 5 minutes. Serve warm or at room temperature.

Lemon Skillet Scones

MAKES 8 SCONES

If you were going to name the official scone of spring, what would it taste like? To us, the fresh flavor of lemon would be ideal, and this rich scone is delightfully seasoned with just the perfect amount. We think a springtime garden luncheon or tea would be the perfect backdrop for these scones. Or, for a classic dessert with a fresh flavor, serve them topped with berries and whipped cream.

Pastry blender (optional)
10-inch (25 cm) cast-iron skillet

SCONES

2¼ cups (560 mL) all-purpose flour (approx.)

½ cup (125 mL) granulated sugar

1 tbsp (15 mL) baking powder

½ tsp (2 mL) salt

2 tsp (10 mL) grated lemon zest

½ cup (125 mL) cold unsalted butter, cubed

⅔ cup + 1 tbsp (165 mL) heavy or whipping (35%) cream (approx.), divided

1 large egg, at room temperature

2 tbsp (30 mL) freshly squeezed lemon juice

1 tbsp (15 mL) coarse white sparkling sugar or turbinado sugar

LEMON GLAZE

½ cup (125 mL) confectioners' (icing) sugar

1½ tbsp (22 mL) freshly squeezed lemon juice

1 **SCONES** Preheat the oven to 425°F (220°C).

2 In a large bowl, whisk together flour, sugar, baking powder and salt. Stir in lemon zest. Using a pastry blender or two knives, cut in cold butter until pea-size pieces form.

3 In a small bowl, whisk together ⅔ cup (150 mL) cream, egg and lemon juice. Pour over the flour mixture and stir gently to make a soft dough. You may need to add up to 2 tbsp (30 mL) more cream. With lightly floured hands, gather dough into a ball in the bowl. Transfer dough to a lightly floured surface. Using both hands, pat into a 9-inch (23 cm) disk about ¾ inch (2 cm) thick. Cut disk in half and cut each half into 4 to yield 8 wedges. Gently lift wedges with a spatula and place in a circle in the skillet. Brush the tops with the remaining 1 tbsp (15 mL) cream and sprinkle with coarse sugar.

4 Bake in the preheated oven for 20 to 25 minutes or until golden.

5 **LEMON GLAZE** In a small bowl, whisk together confectioners' sugar and lemon juice. Set aside.

6 Remove skillet from the oven and place on a wire rack. Lightly spread glaze over the warm scones. Let cool for 5 minutes. If needed, use a sharp knife to cut the wedges apart. Using a heatproof spatula, gently lift each scone from skillet and place on a wire rack. Serve warm.

White Chocolate–Drizzled Peppermint Scones

MAKES 6 SCONES

These scones are delicious all year round, but we recommend baking several batches during the holiday season. Place the scones in festive tins and deliver them to friends and family.

Pastry blender (optional)
10-inch (25 cm) cast-iron skillet
Electric mixer

PEPPERMINT SCONES

2 cups (500 mL) all-purpose flour (approx.)

¼ cup (60 mL) granulated sugar

1 tbsp (15 mL) baking powder

1 tsp (5 mL) salt

¼ cup (60 mL) cold unsalted butter, cubed

1 cup + 1 tbsp (265 mL) cold heavy or whipping (35%) cream, divided

½ tsp (2 mL) vanilla extract

½ tsp (2 mL) peppermint extract

½ cup + 2 tbsp (155 mL) crushed soft peppermint candies, divided (see Tip)

1 tbsp (15 mL) coarse white sparkling sugar or turbinado sugar

WHITE CHOCOLATE DRIZZLE

2 oz (60 g) white chocolate, finely chopped

1 tbsp (15 mL) heavy or whipping (35%) cream

⅓ cup (75 mL) confectioners' (icing) sugar

1½ tbsp (22 mL) unsalted butter, softened and cut into 4 pieces

¼ tsp (1 mL) vanilla extract

1 **PEPPERMINT SCONES** Preheat the oven to 400°F (200°C).

2 In a large bowl, whisk together flour, sugar, baking powder and salt. Using a pastry blender or two knives, cut in cold butter until pea-size pieces form.

3 In a small bowl, combine 1 cup (250 mL) cream, vanilla and peppermint extract. Add to flour mixture and stir until the flour is moistened and no dry flour remains. Gently stir in ½ cup (125 mL) crushed peppermint candies.

4 With lightly floured hands, gather dough into a ball in the bowl. Be sure to form the mixture into a cohesive dough and that all the ingredients are incorporated. Transfer dough to a lightly floured surface. Pat into a 7- or 8-inch (18 to 20 cm) disk about 1 inch (2.5 cm) thick. Cut disk in half and cut each half into 3 to yield 6 wedges. Place in skillet. Brush with remaining 1 tbsp (15 mL) cream and sprinkle with coarse sugar. Bake in the preheated oven for 22 to 25 minutes or until golden brown.

5 Remove skillet from the oven, place on a wire rack and let cool for 10 minutes. If needed, use a sharp knife to cut wedges apart.

6 WHITE CHOCOLATE DRIZZLE
Meanwhile, in a medium microwave-safe bowl, combine white chocolate and cream. Microwave on High for 30 seconds. Add confectioners' sugar, butter and vanilla. Using an electric mixer at medium-high speed, beat until smooth. Top scones with drizzle and sprinkle with remaining 2 tbsp (30 mL) crushed peppermint candies.

TIP | This recipe will not work with hard candies. Use soft peppermint candies.

PIES

Southern Pecan Pie

Calling all bourbon fans! You'll get a double dose here with bourbon-flavored pecans and an infused whipped cream topping. It's the perfect pie to enjoy year-round.

10-inch (25 cm) cast-iron skillet
Electric mixer

10-inch (25 cm) unbaked Single Deep-Dish Pie Crust (page 150), prepared through Step 3

3 large eggs, at room temperature

¾ cup (175 mL) dark corn syrup

¼ cup (60 mL) light corn syrup

⅔ cup (150 mL) packed dark brown sugar

¼ cup (60 mL) unsalted butter, melted and cooled slightly

1 tbsp (15 mL) bourbon

¼ tsp (1 mL) salt

1¾ cups (425 mL) coarsely chopped pecans

BOURBON WHIPPED CREAM

1 cup (250 mL) heavy or whipping (35%) cream

2 tbsp (30 mL) confectioners' (icing) sugar

1 tsp (5 mL) bourbon

1 Preheat the oven to 350°F (180°C).

2 In a large bowl, whisk eggs. Add dark corn syrup, light corn syrup, brown sugar, melted butter, bourbon and salt.

3 Sprinkle pecans evenly over the prepared pie crust. Pour syrup mixture over the pecans.

4 Bake in the preheated oven for 50 to 60 minutes or until a tester inserted in the center comes out clean.

5 Remove skillet from the oven and place on a wire rack. Let pie cool to room temperature before serving.

6 **BOURBON WHIPPED CREAM** Just before serving, in a small, deep bowl, using an electric mixer at medium-high speed, beat cream until frothy. Gradually beat in confectioners' sugar and whip until stiff peaks form. Beat in bourbon until combined. Dollop whipped cream over each piece of pie.

> TIP | If desired, sprinkle ½ cup (125 mL) mini semisweet chocolate chips over the pecans before adding the syrup mixture in Step 3. Proceed with the recipe as directed.

Skillet Apple Pie with Calvados Glaze

MAKES 12 SERVINGS

This pie is so good you can leave off the glaze if you prefer.

10-inch (25 cm) cast-iron skillet

Rimmed baking sheet lined with foil or parchment paper

10-inch (25 cm) unbaked Double Pie Crust (page 151), prepared through Step 3

1 cup + 1 tbsp (265 mL) granulated sugar, divided

⅓ cup (75 mL) cornstarch

¼ cup (60 mL) packed dark brown sugar

2 tsp (10 mL) ground cinnamon

½ tsp (2 mL) salt

13 to 14 cups (3.25 to 3.5 L) peeled, cored and sliced Granny Smith apples (about 4½ lbs/2.25 kg)

2 tbsp (30 mL) Calvados or apple brandy, divided

1 tbsp (15 mL) unsalted butter, cubed

CALVADOS GLAZE

3 tbsp (45 mL) unsalted butter

½ cup (125 mL) packed brown sugar

2 tbsp (30 mL) granulated sugar

⅓ cup (75 mL) heavy or whipping (35%) cream

2 tbsp (30 mL) Calvados or apple brandy

1 Preheat the oven to 400°F (200°C).

2 In a medium bowl, whisk together 1 cup (250 mL) sugar, cornstarch, brown sugar, cinnamon and salt. Set aside.

3 In a large bowl, combine apples and 1 tbsp (15 mL) Calvados; toss to coat. Spoon apples into prepared pie crust, arranging the slices tightly. Sprinkle with sugar mixture. Dot with butter.

4 Unfold top crust over the fruit. Using kitchen scissors, trim off any excess. Flute the edges to seal both crusts to the sides of the skillet, by pressing the pastry between the thumb of one hand and the thumb and index finger of the other. Using a sharp knife, cut 6 slits in the top crust. Brush top crust with remaining 1 tbsp (15 mL) Calvados, then sprinkle with the remaining 1 tbsp (15 mL) granulated sugar.

5 Place the skillet on the prepared baking sheet. Bake in the preheated oven for 1 hour and 10 minutes to 1 hour and 15 minutes, or until the crust is golden brown and the apples are tender.

6 Remove skillet from the oven and place on a wire rack. Let pie cool for 1 hour before slicing.

7 **CALVADOS GLAZE** Just before serving, in a small saucepan, heat butter over medium heat until melted. Stir in brown sugar and granulated sugar and stir until dissolved. Add cream and cook, stirring constantly, for 2 minutes. Remove from heat and stir in Calvados. Place pieces of pie on individual serving plates and drizzle with the Calvados glaze.

Cranberry–Orange Cream Streusel Pie

MAKES 12 SERVINGS

A sweet yet tart ruby-red cranberry sauce contrasts with a creamy orange-flavored filling in this exceptional showstopping pie.

10-inch (25 cm) cast-iron skillet

10-inch (25 cm) unbaked Single Deep-Dish Pie Crust (page 150), prepared through Step 3

CRANBERRY SAUCE

3 cups (750 mL) fresh or frozen cranberries

¾ cup + 2 tbsp (205 mL) granulated sugar

2 tsp (10 mL) grated orange zest

¼ cup (60 mL) orange juice

¼ cup (60 mL) water

CREAMY ORANGE FILLING

1 can (14 oz/300 mL) sweetened condensed milk

1½ tsp (7 mL) grated orange zest

¾ cup (175 mL) orange juice

½ cup (125 mL) unsalted butter, melted

¼ tsp (1 mL) salt

4 large eggs, at room temperature

STREUSEL

1 cup (250 mL) all-purpose flour

⅓ cup (75 mL) granulated sugar

½ tsp (2 mL) ground cinnamon

⅓ cup (75 mL) unsalted butter, melted

1 Preheat the oven to 375°F (190°C).

2 **CRANBERRY SAUCE** In a medium saucepan, combine cranberries, sugar, orange zest, orange juice and water.

Heat mixture over medium-high heat until boiling. Reduce heat and simmer, stirring occasionally, for 15 minutes or until the skins of the cranberries pop. Let cool for 1 hour.

3 **CREAMY ORANGE FILLING** Meanwhile, in a large bowl, whisk together condensed milk, orange zest, orange juice, melted butter and salt. Whisk in eggs one a time, whisking well after each addition.

4 Pour filling mixture into the prepared pie crust. Bake in the preheated oven for 35 minutes or until the filling is set at the edges but soft in the center.

5 Remove skillet from the oven and place on a wire rack.

6 **STREUSEL** Meanwhile, in a small bowl, combine flour, sugar and cinnamon. Add melted butter and stir until crumbly.

7 Spoon cranberry sauce gently over the orange filling. Sprinkle with streusel mixture. Bake for 25 to 30 minutes more or until golden brown. Remove skillet from the oven and place on a wire rack. Let pie cool for 1 hour before slicing.

> **TIP** | If desired, substitute 1 can (14 oz/ 398 mL) whole-berry cranberry sauce for the cranberry sauce in this recipe.

Deep-Dish Cherry Pie

MAKES 12 SERVINGS

Who doesn't smile when they hear "Cherry pie for dessert"? We prefer cherry pies prepared in the cast-iron skillet because it is deeper than a traditional pie plate and can hold extra cherries. Of course, you can always embellish each serving with a scoop of vanilla ice cream.

10-inch (25 cm) cast-iron skillet

Rimmed baking sheet lined with foil or parchment paper

10-inch (25 cm) unbaked Double Pie Crust (page 151), prepared through Step 3

7 cups (1.75 L) fresh or frozen pitted tart cherries (thawed if frozen)

½ cup (125 mL) granulated sugar

½ cup (125 mL) packed dark brown sugar

¼ cup (60 mL) cornstarch

1 tsp (5 mL) almond extract

⅛ tsp (0.5 mL) salt

1 large egg, at room temperature

1 tbsp (15 mL) water

1 tbsp (15 mL) coarse white sparkling sugar or turbinado sugar

Vanilla ice cream (optional)

1 Preheat the oven to 425°F (220°C).

2 In a medium saucepan, gently stir together cherries, granulated sugar, brown sugar and cornstarch. Cook over medium-high heat, stirring constantly, until mixture begins to simmer. Continue to simmer, stirring constantly, until the mixture thickens, about 5 to 7 minutes. Remove from the heat. Add almond extract and salt; stir to combine. Spoon into prepared pie crust.

3 Unfold top crust over the fruit. Using kitchen scissors, trim off any excess. Flute the sides to seal both crusts to the edges of the skillet, by pressing the pastry between the thumb of one hand and the thumb and index finger of the other. Using a sharp knife, cut 6 slits in the top crust.

4 In a small bowl, whisk together egg and water. Brush top crust with the egg mixture, then sprinkle with coarse sugar. Place skillet on the prepared baking sheet.

5 Bake in the preheated oven for 15 minutes, then reduce the oven temperature to 375°F (190°C) and continue to bake for 35 to 40 minutes more, until crust is brown and filling is bubbling.

6 Remove skillet from the oven and place on a wire rack. Let pie cool before slicing. Serve warm or at room temperature with a scoop of vanilla ice cream (if using) on top.

> **TIP** | Do not substitute sweet cherries (such as Bing) for the tart cherries in this recipe.

Dark Chocolate S'mores Pie

MAKES 12 SERVINGS

In this recipe, campfire s'mores become an elegant, showstopping dessert. The pie is layered with dark chocolate, a marshmallow meringue, a sprinkling of graham cracker crumbs and a drizzle of dark chocolate syrup. Decadent, if you ask us!

10-inch (25 cm) cast-iron skillet
Electric mixer

S'MORES PIE

10-inch (25 cm) unbaked Single Deep-Dish Pie Crust (page 150), prepared through Step 3

1 cup (250 mL) unsalted butter, cubed

4 oz (125 g) 60% to 80% bittersweet (dark) chocolate

2 cups (500 mL) granulated sugar

4 large eggs, at room temperature

1 large egg yolk, at room temperature

1½ cups (375 mL) all-purpose flour

⅓ cup (75 mL) unsweetened cocoa powder

½ tsp (2 mL) salt

1½ tsp (7 mL) vanilla extract

MARSHMALLOW MERINGUE

4 large egg whites, at room temperature

1 tsp (5 mL) cream of tartar

Pinch salt

¼ cup (60 mL) granulated sugar

1 jar (7 oz/198 g) marshmallow crème

1 tbsp (15 mL) graham cracker crumbs

2 tbsp (30 mL) store-bought dark chocolate syrup

1 S'MORES PIE Preheat the oven to 350°F (180°C).

2 In a medium saucepan, combine butter and chocolate. Heat over low heat, stirring frequently, until melted. Remove from heat and let cool for 3 minutes.

3 Whisk sugar into the chocolate mixture. Add eggs, one at a time, and egg yolk, whisking well after each addition. Continue whisking until the mixture turns glossy. Add flour, cocoa powder and salt; whisk just until combined. Whisk in vanilla. Spoon into prepared pie crust.

4 Bake in the preheated oven for 50 to 60 minutes, until the filling is set and a tester inserted in the center comes out with just a few crumbs attached.

5 MARSHMALLOW MERINGUE When the baking time for the pie has 10 minutes left, start the meringue. In a large bowl, using an electric mixer at medium-high speed, beat egg whites, cream of tartar and salt until frothy. Add sugar and continue beating until soft peaks form. Add marshmallow crème one large spoonful at a time; beat at high speed after each addition until the mixture is very smooth and stiff peaks form.

6 Remove pie from oven and spoon meringue over it, taking care to cover it completely, to the edges of the crust. Return pie to the oven and bake for 10 to 15 minutes, until the peaks of the meringue are golden brown.

7 Remove pie from the oven and let cool on a wire rack for 30 minutes before slicing and serving. Garnish with graham cracker crumbs and a drizzle of chocolate syrup.

Brown Butter Sweet Potato Pie

MAKES 12 SERVINGS

Many of us have fond memories of Grandma's sweet potato pie at family celebrations and holidays. In the southern United States this pie replaces pumpkin pie at many a Thanksgiving table. It is usually enjoyed with a dollop of sweetened whipped cream on top.

Rimmed baking sheet lined with parchment paper

Stand mixer

10-inch (25 cm) cast-iron skillet

10-inch (25 cm) unbaked Single Deep-Dish Pie Crust (page 150), prepared through Step 3

2 medium sweet potatoes (about 1½ lbs/750 g)

3 tbsp (45 mL) unsalted butter, thinly sliced

½ tsp (2 mL) ground cinnamon

½ tsp (2 mL) salt

¼ tsp (1 mL) ground nutmeg

2 large eggs, at room temperature

1 can (14 oz/300 mL) sweetened condensed milk

2 tsp (10 mL) freshly squeezed lemon juice

1 Preheat the oven to 400°F (200°C).

2 Place sweet potatoes on the prepared baking sheet. Prick the potatoes about 5 times with a fork. Roast for about 1 hour or until tender. Remove from the oven and place on a wire rack to cool slightly.

3 Reduce oven temperature to 350°F (180°C).

4 In a small saucepan, heat butter over medium heat until melted. Continue cooking until slightly brown, about 2 to 3 minutes. Remove from heat and stir in cinnamon, salt and nutmeg. Set aside.

5 Once the sweet potatoes are cool enough to handle, peel and cut them into medium chunks. Place in the bowl of the stand mixer fitted with the paddle attachment. Beat at medium speed for 2 minutes or until potato is smooth. Add eggs one at a time, beating well after each addition. Add the browned butter, making sure to scrape any brown bits into the bowl, condensed milk and lemon juice. Beat until combined.

6 Pour sweet potato mixture into the prepared pie crust. Bake in the preheated oven for 45 to 50 minutes or until a tester inserted in the center comes out clean.

7 Remove from the oven and place on a wire rack. Let pie cool for 1 hour before slicing. Serve at room temperature.

Peach Crostata

MAKES 12 SERVINGS

What exactly is a crostata? Typically it's a rolled-out piece of pastry that has been piled with fruit or vegetables. The edges of the dough are folded in over the filling, leaving the center open, and it's baked until golden. A crostata and a galette are the same thing, but a crostata is Italian and a galette is French. Either term is acceptable, and both are equally delicious!

10-inch (25 cm) cast-iron skillet

10-inch (25 cm) unbaked Single Deep-Dish Pie Crust (page 150), prepared through Step 2

8 cups (2 L) sliced peeled fresh or frozen peaches

¾ cup (175 mL) packed dark brown sugar

¼ cup (60 mL) cornstarch

2 tbsp (30 mL) crystallized ginger, finely chopped

1 tbsp (15 mL) freshly squeezed lemon juice

½ tsp (2 mL) ground cinnamon

¼ tsp (1 mL) ground nutmeg

½ cup (125 mL) water

⅛ tsp (0.5 mL) salt

1 In a large bowl, combine peaches, brown sugar, cornstarch, crystallized ginger, lemon juice, cinnamon and nutmeg. Let stand at room temperature for 1 hour, stirring twice to meld flavors.

2 Preheat the oven to 400°F (200°C).

3 On a lightly floured surface, using a floured rolling pin, roll out pie crust to form a 13-inch (33 cm) circle. Gently fold dough into quarters and transfer to the skillet. Unfold, lining the skillet evenly across the bottom and up the sides. Make sure to gently push the pastry down into the skillet.

4 Using a slotted spoon, lift peaches out of the bowl, allowing the liquid to drain off into the bowl, and place peaches in the pastry-lined skillet. Set aside bowl of liquid.

5 Fold edges of the pie crust over the filling, leaving the center uncovered (the edges will look pleated). Bake in the preheated oven for 55 to 65 minutes or until the crust is golden brown and the filling is bubbling.

6 Remove skillet from the oven and place on a wire rack. Let crostata cool for 45 minutes before slicing.

7 Just before serving, in a small saucepan, combine reserved peach liquid, water and salt. Cook over medium-high heat, stirring constantly, until thickened, about 3 to 5 minutes. Place pieces of the crostata on individual serving plates and drizzle with the peach sauce.

> TIP | The crystallized ginger can be omitted for more of a traditional peach pie flavor.

Butterscotch Pumpkin Pie

MAKES 12 SERVINGS

For many people, it's not possible to host Thanksgiving or a big autumn dinner without a pumpkin pie. While this is a traditional recipe, the butterscotch sauce gives it a sweet, buttery twist that makes the flavor soar.

10-inch (25 cm) cast-iron skillet
Electric mixer

10-inch (25 cm) unbaked Single Deep-Dish Pie Crust (page 150), prepared through Step 3

BUTTERSCOTCH SAUCE

¼ cup (60 mL) unsalted butter, thinly sliced

¾ cup (175 mL) packed brown sugar

¼ cup (60 mL) granulated sugar

1 cup (250 mL) heavy or whipping (35%) cream

PUMPKIN PIE

4 large eggs, at room temperature

1 tsp (5 mL) ground ginger

1 tsp (5 mL) ground cinnamon

½ tsp (2 mL) ground nutmeg

½ tsp (2 mL) salt

1 can (15 oz/442 mL) pumpkin purée

1 can (12 oz/370 mL) evaporated milk

TOPPING

1 cup (250 mL) heavy or whipping (35%) cream

1 Preheat the oven to 400°F (200°C).

2 BUTTERSCOTCH SAUCE In a small saucepan, heat butter over medium heat until melted. Add brown sugar and granulated sugar; cook, stirring frequently, for 2 minutes or until mixture is bubbling. Stir in cream and heat, stirring constantly, until boiling. Remove from heat and let cool for 10 minutes. Once cool, reserve ⅔ cup (150 mL) sauce for serving. Set aside.

3 PUMPKIN PIE Meanwhile, in a large bowl, whisk together eggs, ginger, cinnamon, nutmeg and salt. Add pumpkin purée and evaporated milk; whisk until smooth.

4 Add remaining butterscotch sauce to the pumpkin mixture and whisk until smooth. Pour the mixture into the prepared pie crust.

5 Bake in the preheated oven for 50 minutes or until a tester inserted off-center comes out clean. (The center will still be softly set and jiggly, but it will continue to set as it cools.) Remove skillet from the oven and place on a wire rack. Let pie cool for 1 hour.

6 TOPPING Just before serving, in a small, deep bowl, using an electric mixer at medium-high speed, beat cream until stiff peaks form. Dollop spoonfuls of whipped cream in a decorative fashion around outside edges of pie. Cut pie into pieces and drizzle each with reserved butterscotch sauce.

> **TIP** | Substitute 2½ tsp (12 mL) pumpkin pie spice for the ginger, cinnamon and nutmeg.

Single Deep-Dish Pie Crust

MAKES ONE 10-INCH (25 CM) PIE CRUST

This pie-crust recipe will quickly become your go-to anytime you're thinking pie. Most pies, such as Southern Pecan Pie (page 139) and Dark Chocolate S'mores Pie (page 145), need only a bottom crust, and this is the ideal recipe to use.

Pastry blender (optional)
10-inch (25 cm) cast-iron skillet

1½ cups (375 mL) all-purpose flour (approx.)

½ tsp (2 mL) salt

½ cup + 1 tbsp (140 mL) shortening (see Tip)

6 to 8 tbsp (90 to 120 mL) ice water (approx.)

1 In a large bowl, whisk together flour and salt. Using a pastry blender or two knives, cut in shortening until pea-size pieces form. Drizzle with 6 tbsp (90 mL) water and let stand for 30 seconds. Mix lightly with a fork until dough holds together and cleans the sides of the bowl. Add more ice water, 1 tbsp (15 mL) at a time, if necessary.

2 Gather dough into a ball. Shape into a disk and wrap in plastic wrap. Refrigerate for at least 30 minutes or up to 24 hours.

3 On a lightly floured surface, using a floured rolling pin, roll out the dough to form a circle about 14 inches (35 cm) in diameter. Gently fold the dough into quarters and transfer to the skillet. Unfold, lining the skillet evenly across the bottom and up the sides. Make sure to gently push the pastry down into the skillet. Using kitchen scissors, trim off any excess. Flute the edges to seal the crust to the sides of the skillet by pressing the pastry between the thumb of one hand and the thumb and index finger of the other.

4 **FOR UNBAKED PIE CRUST** Use as directed in the recipe.

FOR BAKED PIE CRUST Preheat the oven to 425°F (220°C). Prick the bottom and sides of the crust with the tines of a fork. Bake in the preheated oven for 10 to 12 minutes or until lightly browned. Let cool completely before filling.

> TIP | If desired, substitute cold unsalted butter for half of the shortening. While an all-shortening crust is often easier to work with, some people prefer the flavor that butter imparts.

Double Pie Crust

Cast-iron skillets are known for making great pies. Use this basic double-crust recipe for any of your favorite cast-iron pies that have a bottom and top crust, such as Skillet Apple Pie with Calvados Glaze (page 140) or Deep-Dish Cherry Pie (page 142).

Pastry blender (optional)
10-inch (25 cm) cast-iron skillet

2⅔ cups (650 mL) all-purpose flour

1 tsp (5 mL) salt

1 cup (250 mL) shortening

9 to 11 tbsp (135 to 165 mL) ice water

1 In a large bowl, whisk together flour and salt. Using a pastry blender or two knives, cut in shortening until pea-size pieces form. Drizzle with 9 tbsp (135 mL) water and let stand for 30 seconds. Mix lightly with a fork until dough holds together and cleans the sides of the bowl. Add more ice water, 1 tbsp (15 mL) at a time, if necessary.

2 Gather dough into a ball. Divide dough into 2 portions: one portion should use about ⅔ of the dough and the other should be the remaining ⅓ of the dough. Shape each portion into a disk and wrap in plastic wrap. Refrigerate for at least 30 minutes or up to 24 hours.

3 On a lightly floured work surface, using a floured rolling pin, roll out the larger portion to form a circle about 14 inches (35 cm) in diameter. Gently fold the rolled dough into quarters and transfer to the skillet. Unfold, lining the skillet evenly across the bottom and up the sides. Make sure to gently push the pastry down into the skillet. Roll out the smaller portion of dough into a 10- to 12-inch (25 to 30 cm) circle. Gently fold the smaller circle into quarters and set aside.

4 Fill the bottom crust and place the top crust over the filling as the recipe directs. Using kitchen scissors, trim off any excess. Flute the edges to seal the crusts to the sides of the skillet by pressing the pastry between the thumb of one hand and the thumb and index finger of the other. Using a knife, cut 5 slits in the top crust. Bake as directed.

COOKIES AND BROWNIES

Crackle Caramel Brownies

MAKES 16 SERVINGS

Roxanne has fond memories of enjoying these caramel-filled chocolate brownies at almost every family gathering and celebration, and she still enjoys them today.

10-inch (25 cm) cast-iron skillet lined with a 15-inch (38 cm) square of parchment paper

40 individually wrapped chewy caramel candies, unwrapped

$^2/_3$ cup (150 mL) evaporated milk, divided

1 package (15.25 to 18 oz/432 to 560 g) German chocolate cake mix or chocolate cake mix

$^2/_3$ cup (150 mL) unsalted butter, melted

$^1/_2$ cup (125 mL) semisweet chocolate chips

$^3/_4$ cup (175 mL) chopped toasted pecans (see page 21)

1 Preheat the oven to 350°F (180°C).

2 In a medium microwave-safe bowl, combine caramel candies and $^1/_3$ cup (75 mL) evaporated milk. Microwave on High in 45-second intervals, stirring in between, until the candies are melted and the mixture is smooth. Set aside.

3 In a large bowl, stir together cake mix, melted butter and remaining $^1/_3$ cup (75 mL) evaporated milk. Press half of the mixture evenly into the bottom of the prepared skillet. Bake in the preheated oven for 8 minutes.

4 Remove skillet from the oven and place on a wire rack. Sprinkle chocolate chips evenly over the crust. Stir pecans into the caramel mixture and spoon evenly over the chocolate chips. Dollop remaining cake mix batter evenly over the caramel mixture.

5 Bake for 25 to 30 minutes or until the entire brownie is set and cooked through.

6 Remove skillet from the oven and place on a wire rack. Let cool for 30 minutes. Carefully, using the edges of the parchment paper, lift brownie out of the skillet and place on a wire rack. Let cool completely. Cut into squares.

> **TIP** | For a smooth caramel filling, omit the pecans.

Swirl Brownies

MAKES 16 SERVINGS

The crispy edges of the brownie and an inviting rich cream cheese swirl pair perfectly to create a delicious no-fuss treat.

Electric mixer

10-inch (25 cm) cast-iron skillet lined with a 15-inch (38 cm) square of parchment paper

1 cup (250 mL) all-purpose flour

3 tbsp (45 mL) unsweetened cocoa powder

¼ tsp (1 mL) salt

10 tbsp (150 mL) unsalted butter, thinly sliced

½ cup (125 mL) semisweet chocolate chips

1 cup (250 mL) granulated sugar

2 large eggs, at room temperature

1 tsp (5 mL) vanilla extract

CREAM CHEESE SWIRL

8 oz (250 g) cream cheese, softened

¼ cup (60 mL) granulated sugar

⅛ tsp (0.5 mL) salt

1 large egg, at room temperature

2 tsp (10 mL) vanilla extract

CANDY BAR FROSTING

3 bars (each 1.55 oz/43 g) milk chocolate candy, cut into ½-inch (1 cm) pieces (see Tip)

1 Preheat the oven to 325°F (160°C).

2 In a small bowl, whisk together flour, cocoa powder and salt. Set aside.

3 In a medium microwave-safe bowl, combine butter and chocolate chips. Microwave on High in 45-second intervals, stirring in between, until the mixture is melted and smooth. Set aside.

4 In a large bowl, using an electric mixer at medium-high speed, combine sugar, eggs and vanilla. Add butter mixture and beat until combined. Add flour mixture and beat until just combined. Spoon into prepared skillet and smooth the batter evenly. Set aside.

5 **CREAM CHEESE SWIRL** In a medium bowl, using an electric mixer at medium-high speed, beat cream cheese, sugar, salt, egg and vanilla until smooth. Dollop evenly over batter in the skillet. Using a table knife, gently lift the brownie batter over the cream cheese mixture just until swirled. Do not over-swirl.

6 Bake in the preheated oven for 45 to 50 minutes or until set and a tester inserted in the center comes out clean.

7 **CANDY BAR FROSTING** Remove skillet from the oven and place on a wire rack. Immediately sprinkle the pieces of chocolate bar over the hot brownie. Cover with a sheet of aluminum foil and let stand for 5 minutes. Uncover and frost by spreading the chocolate evenly over the brownie. Let stand until frosting sets and is firm. Carefully, using the edges of the parchment paper, lift brownie out of the skillet and place on a wire rack. Cut into bars.

> TIP | If you desire, do not frost these brownies. They are delicious and attractive enough to serve unfrosted.

Dark Chocolate Fudge Brownies

If you are someone who enjoys dense, fudgy brownies, then this is the recipe for you. Let them cool completely, then cut into delicious pieces. However, if you want a rich, chocolate dessert with maximum fudge, you could serve while still a bit warm from the skillet.

10-inch (25 cm) cast-iron skillet lined with a 15-inch (38 cm) square of parchment paper

1 cup (250 mL) all-purpose flour

½ tsp (2 mL) salt

1 cup (250 mL) unsalted butter, thinly sliced

8 oz (250 g) 60% to 80% bittersweet (dark) chocolate, finely chopped

1⅔ cups (400 mL) granulated sugar

2 tbsp (30 mL) unsweetened cocoa powder

4 large eggs, at room temperature

1 tsp (5 mL) vanilla extract

½ cup (125 mL) chopped toasted walnuts or pecans (optional; see page 21)

1 Preheat the oven to 350°F (180°C).

2 In a medium bowl, whisk together flour and salt. Set aside.

3 In a medium saucepan over low heat, melt butter and chocolate. Whisk until smooth. Remove from the heat. Whisk in sugar and cocoa powder until smooth. Whisk in eggs one a time, whisking well after each addition. Whisk in flour mixture until combined. Whisk in vanilla. Stir in walnuts (if using). Spoon into the prepared skillet.

4 Bake in the preheated oven for 45 to 50 minutes or until a tester inserted in the center comes out with a few crumbs attached.

5 Remove skillet from the oven and place on a wire rack. Let cool for 30 minutes. Carefully, using the edges of the parchment paper, lift brownie out of the skillet and place on a wire rack. Let cool completely. Cut into bars.

Peanut Butter Brownies

MAKES 16 SERVINGS

These peanut butter brownies are rich, buttery and packed with peanut flavor. Take a few to work for a snack or take some along on a picnic.

10-inch (25 cm) cast-iron skillet lined with a 15-inch (38 cm) square of parchment paper

1¼ cups (310 mL) all-purpose flour

½ tsp (2 mL) baking powder

½ tsp (2 mL) salt

¼ tsp (1 mL) baking soda

¾ cup (175 mL) unsalted butter, thinly sliced

1 cup (250 mL) packed dark brown sugar

¾ cup (175 mL) granulated sugar

1 cup (250 mL) creamy peanut butter

2 large eggs, at room temperature

2 tsp (10 mL) vanilla extract

½ cup (125 mL) dry-roasted peanuts, chopped

½ cup (125 mL) peanut butter chips

1 Preheat the oven to 350°F (180°C).

2 In a medium bowl, whisk together flour, baking powder, salt and baking soda. Set aside.

3 In a medium saucepan over medium heat, melt the butter. Whisk in brown sugar and granulated sugar. Cook, whisking constantly, for 1 minute or until combined and sugars are dissolved. Remove from the heat. Whisk in peanut butter until smooth. Whisk in eggs one a time, whisking well after each addition. Whisk in the vanilla. Stir in the flour mixture. Stir in the peanuts and peanut butter chips. Spoon into the prepared skillet.

4 Bake in the preheated oven for 40 to 45 minutes or until a tester inserted in the center comes out with a few crumbs attached.

5 Remove skillet from the oven and place on a wire rack. Let cool for 30 minutes. Carefully, using the edges of the parchment paper, lift brownie out of the skillet and place on a wire rack. Let cool completely. Cut into bars.

> **TIP** | Substitute semisweet chocolate chips for the peanut butter chips, if desired.

Butterscotch Blondies

MAKES 16 SERVINGS

Blondies are "blonde" brownies, since they do not contain cocoa powder. This recipe has a rich butterscotch flavor and gets a little crunch from toasted pecans. Of course, if you are a die-hard chocoholic, you can replace the butterscotch chips with semisweet chocolate chips.

Electric mixer

10-inch (25 cm) cast-iron skillet lined with a 15-inch (38 cm) square of parchment paper

1½ cups (375 mL) all-purpose flour

1½ tsp (7 mL) baking powder

½ tsp (2 mL) kosher salt

1½ cups (375 mL) packed dark brown sugar

½ cup (125 mL) unsalted butter, softened

2 large eggs, at room temperature

2 tsp (10 mL) vanilla extract

1 cup (250 mL) chopped toasted pecans (see page 21)

1 cup (250 mL) butterscotch chips

1 Preheat the oven to 350°F (180°C).

2 In a medium bowl, whisk together flour, baking powder and salt. Set aside.

3 In a large bowl, using an electric mixer at medium-high speed, beat brown sugar and butter until light and fluffy, about 3 minutes. Add eggs and vanilla and continue to beat for 1 minute. With the mixer at low speed, add flour mixture, beating until combined. Stir in the pecans and butterscotch chips. Spoon into the prepared skillet.

4 Bake in the preheated oven for 30 to 35 minutes or until a tester inserted in the center comes out with a few crumbs attached.

5 Remove skillet from the oven and place on a wire rack. Let cool for 30 minutes. Carefully, using the edges of the parchment paper, lift blondie out of the skillet and place on a wire rack. Let cool completely. Cut into bars.

> TIP | For extra butterscotch flavor, omit the pecans and increase the quantity of butterscotch chips to 2 cups (500 mL). Proceed with the recipe as directed.

Toffee Skillet Blondie

MAKES 16 SERVINGS

Invite a friend to sit at your kitchen table and enjoy a cup of coffee and a slice of this blondie. It's the simple pleasures like these that we must cherish. And have a recipe card ready, because your friend will definitely be asking for it!

Electric mixer
10-inch (25 cm) cast-iron skillet

1 cup + 2 tbsp (280 mL) all-purpose flour

¾ tsp (3 mL) baking powder

½ tsp (2 mL) baking soda

½ tsp (2 mL) salt

6 tbsp (90 mL) unsalted butter, melted

1 cup (250 mL) packed dark brown sugar

2 large eggs, at room temperature

2 tsp (10 mL) vanilla extract

8 oz (250 g) milk chocolate toffee bits

3 tbsp (45 mL) unsalted butter, softened and thinly sliced

1 Preheat the oven to 350°F (180°C).

2 In a medium bowl, whisk together flour, baking powder, baking soda and salt. Set aside.

3 In a large bowl, using an electric mixer at medium-high speed, beat together melted butter, brown sugar, eggs and vanilla until combined. Add flour mixture and beat until combined. Stir in toffee bits. Set aside.

4 Place sliced butter in the skillet. Place skillet in the preheated oven for 4 minutes, or just until the butter is melted (watch closely and do not allow butter to brown). Remove skillet from the oven and place on a wire rack. Spoon batter into the skillet.

5 Bake in the preheated oven for 25 to 30 minutes or until a tester inserted in the center comes out with a few crumbs attached.

6 Remove skillet from the oven and place on a wire rack. Let cool completely. Slice blondie into pieces.

TIP | You can omit the toffee bits and substitute semisweet chocolate chips and ½ cup (125 mL) chopped toasted pecans if you prefer. Proceed with the recipe as directed.

Snickerdoodle Bars

MAKES 16 SERVINGS

If you enjoy snickerdoodles, those buttery sugar cookies rolled in cinnamon sugar, then this is the bar for you.

Electric mixer

10-inch (25 cm) cast-iron skillet lined with a 15-inch (38 cm) square of parchment paper

1¾ cups (425 mL) all-purpose flour

1 tsp (5 mL) baking powder

½ tsp (2 mL) salt

1 cup + 1 tbsp (265 mL) granulated sugar, divided

½ cup (125 mL) unsalted butter, softened

⅓ cup (75 mL) packed dark brown sugar

2 large eggs, at room temperature

2 tsp (10 mL) vanilla extract

1 tbsp (15 mL) ground cinnamon

VANILLA ICING

¾ cup (175 mL) confectioners' (icing) sugar

1 tbsp (15 mL) milk

¼ tsp (1 mL) vanilla extract

1 Preheat the oven to 350°F (180°C).

2 In a medium bowl, whisk together flour, baking powder and salt. Set aside.

3 In a large bowl, using an electric mixer at medium-high speed, beat together 1 cup (250 mL) granulated sugar, butter and brown sugar for 2 minutes or until creamy. Beat in eggs one a time, beating well after each addition. Beat in vanilla. Stir in flour mixture.

4 In a small bowl, stir together remaining 1 tbsp (15 mL) sugar and cinnamon.

5 Spoon half of the dough into the prepared skillet and spread evenly. Sprinkle the cinnamon-sugar mixture evenly over the batter. Dollop the remaining dough evenly over the top. Bake in the preheated oven for 40 to 45 minutes or until a tester inserted in the center comes out clean.

6 Remove skillet from the oven and place on a wire rack. Let cool for 30 minutes. Carefully, using the edges of the parchment paper, lift cookie out of the skillet and place on a wire rack. Let cool completely.

7 **VANILLA ICING** Meanwhile, in a small bowl, whisk together confectioners' sugar, milk and vanilla until smooth. Spoon into a small resealable plastic bag (or use a piping bag). Clip a corner off the bag and drizzle the icing decoratively over the cookie. Cut into bars.

> **TIP** | Though not traditional, this bar cookie is also excellent with nuts. Stir ½ cup (125 mL) finely chopped toasted pecans into the cinnamon-sugar mixture in Step 4.

Chocolate Chip Skillet Cookie

MAKES 16 SERVINGS

There's no need to rush to the local grocery or bakery to pick up a cookie cake for a celebration. This recipe comes together in a snap and can be served warm with ice cream, if desired.

Electric mixer

10-inch (25 cm) cast-iron skillet

2 cups + 2 tbsp (530 mL) all-purpose flour

½ tsp (2 mL) baking soda

½ tsp (2 mL) salt

¾ cup (175 mL) unsalted butter, melted and cooled slightly

¾ cup (175 mL) packed dark brown sugar

¾ cup (175 mL) granulated sugar

2 large eggs, at room temperature

1½ tsp (7 mL) vanilla extract

2 cups (500 mL) semisweet chocolate chips

1 tsp (5 mL) unsalted butter, softened

Vanilla ice cream (optional)

1 Preheat the oven to 325°F (160°C).

2 In a medium bowl, whisk together flour, baking soda and salt. Set aside.

3 In a large bowl, using an electric mixer at medium-high speed, beat together melted butter, brown sugar and granulated sugar for 2 minutes or until creamy. Add eggs one at a time, beating after each addition. Beat in vanilla. Stir in flour mixture, just until combined. Stir in chocolate chips.

4 Grease skillet with softened butter. Press cookie dough into the prepared skillet. Bake in the preheated oven for 30 to 35 minutes or until golden brown.

5 Remove skillet from the oven and place on a wire rack. Let cool for 30 minutes. Cut cookie into pieces and serve with a scoop of vanilla ice cream on top (if using).

Oatmeal Raisin Skillet Cookie

MAKES ABOUT 16 SERVINGS

This cast-iron skillet cookie is a comforting, old-fashioned treat. It may bring back delicious childhood memories of one of your favorite cookies, chock-full of raisins and topped with a perfect light glaze.

Electric mixer

10-inch (25 cm) cast-iron skillet

¾ cup (175 mL) all-purpose flour

½ tsp (2 mL) baking soda

½ tsp (2 mL) ground cinnamon

¼ tsp (1 mL) salt

¼ tsp (1 mL) ground nutmeg

¾ cup (175 mL) packed dark brown sugar

½ cup + 1 tsp (130 mL) unsalted butter, softened and divided

1 large egg, at room temperature

1 large egg yolk, at room temperature

2 tbsp (30 mL) milk

1½ cups (375 mL) rolled oats (quick-cooking or large-flake/old-fashioned)

1 cup (250 mL) dark raisins

GLAZE

¾ cup (175 mL) confectioners' (icing) sugar

1 tbsp (15 mL) milk

2 tsp (10 mL) hot water

1 Preheat the oven to 350°F (180°C).

2 In a medium bowl, whisk together flour, baking soda, cinnamon, salt and nutmeg. Set aside.

3 In a large bowl, using an electric mixer at medium-high speed, beat together brown sugar and ½ cup (125 mL) butter until creamy, about 2 minutes. Beat in egg, egg yolk and milk. Stir in flour mixture. Stir in oats and raisins.

4 Grease skillet with remaining 1 tsp (5 mL) softened butter. Spoon dough into the prepared skillet. Bake in the preheated oven for 30 to 35 minutes or until the edges of the cookie are set and beginning to pull away from the skillet.

5 Remove the skillet from the oven and place on a wire rack. Let cool for 30 minutes.

6 **GLAZE** Meanwhile, in a small bowl, whisk together confectioners' sugar, milk and hot water. Drizzle over cookie and, using the back of a spoon, spread to cover evenly. Let cool completely. Cut into pieces.

> **TIP** | Stir in ½ cup (125 mL) chopped toasted pecans along with the oats and raisins in Step 3, if desired.

DESSERTS

Tarte Tatin

MAKES 12 SERVINGS

This is a taste of Paris as fine as any you could purchase at a pastry shop. Once you realize how easy it is to prepare this traditional French dessert, it will become your go-to for easy entertaining.

Baking sheet lined with parchment paper

10-inch (25 cm) cast-iron skillet

All-purpose flour

1 sheet (8 oz/225 g) puff pastry dough, 10 inches (25 cm) square, thawed if frozen (half a 17.3 oz/490 g package)

6 tbsp (90 mL) unsalted butter, softened

¾ cup (175 mL) granulated sugar

⅛ tsp (0.5 mL) kosher salt

2 tbsp (30 mL) freshly squeezed lemon juice

6 Gala or Pink Lady apples, peeled, cored and quartered

1 Preheat the oven to 425°F (220°C).

2 On a lightly floured work surface, unroll puff pastry. Using a floured rolling pin, roll pastry into a 12-inch (30 cm) square. Cut a circle 11 inches (28 cm) in diameter, discarding scraps. (As a guide, invert the skillet over the pastry and cut around it, making the circle a little larger than the skillet.) Place pastry circle on the prepared baking sheet and refrigerate until needed.

3 Spread butter evenly over the bottom of the skillet. Sprinkle sugar evenly over butter. Sprinkle evenly with salt and lemon juice. Place apple quarters in a single layer, cut sides up, over the bottom of the skillet; you may need to lay one or two quarters on top of the first layer. Keep in mind that you invert the skillet to serve, so the bottom will become the top — try to arrange the apples neatly. (Even if the apples seem tightly arranged, they will fit better once cooked.)

4 Heat skillet on the stovetop over medium heat until the sugar melts, caramelizes and thickens, about 20 to 25 minutes. If the mixture starts to get very dark, reduce the heat slightly.

5 Remove puff pastry from the refrigerator. Carefully remove skillet from the heat and place on a wire rack. Place puff pastry circle over the apples; use the edge of a spatula or a butter knife to tuck it down the sides of the skillet. Using a sharp knife, cut 3 or 4 slits in the pastry. Bake in the preheated oven for 20 to 25 minutes, until the pastry is golden.

6 Remove skillet from the oven and place on a wire rack. Let cool for 15 minutes. Place a large platter with raised edges over the skillet. Wearing oven mitts, carefully invert tarte onto the platter. Remove the skillet. Serve tarte warm or at room temperature.

Peach Bourbon Upside-Down Cake

MAKES 9 SERVINGS

A cast-iron skillet perfectly caramelizes the fruit in this upside-down dessert, and the bourbon adds an extra hit of flavor to the delicious peaches. Serve this warm after dinner or for an afternoon treat.

10-inch (25 cm) cast-iron skillet
Electric mixer

1½ cups (375 mL) all-purpose flour

1½ tsp (7 mL) baking powder

¼ tsp (1 mL) salt

¼ tsp (1 mL) ground nutmeg

1 cup (250 mL) unsalted butter, softened and divided

⅔ cup (150 mL) packed light brown sugar (see Tip)

¼ cup (60 mL) bourbon, divided

2¼ cups (560 mL) peeled, sliced fresh or unsweetened frozen peaches (about 4 medium peaches)

1 cup (250 mL) granulated sugar

1 large egg, at room temperature

1 large egg yolk, at room temperature

1 tsp (5 mL) vanilla extract

½ cup (125 mL) milk

1 Preheat the oven to 350°F (180°C).

2 In a medium bowl, whisk together flour, baking powder, salt and nutmeg. Set aside.

3 Thinly slice ⅓ cup (75 mL) butter and place in the skillet. Place skillet in the preheated oven for 4 minutes or just until the butter is melted. (Watch closely and do not allow the butter to brown.)

4 Remove skillet from the oven and place on a wire rack. Stir brown sugar into the butter to moisten. Stir in 3 tbsp (45 mL) bourbon. Spread sugar mixture evenly over bottom of skillet. Arrange peach slices on top.

5 In a large bowl, using an electric mixer at medium-high speed, beat together remaining ⅔ cup (150 mL) butter and granulated sugar until light and fluffy, about 3 minutes. Beat in the egg and egg yolk one a time, beating well after each addition. Beat in vanilla.

6 In a small bowl, stir together milk and remaining 1 tbsp (15 mL) bourbon. With the mixer on low speed, alternately add flour mixture and milk mixture to butter mixture (3 additions of flour and 2 of milk), and beat until smooth. Spoon batter over the peaches.

7 Bake in the preheated oven for 55 to 60 minutes or until a tester inserted in the center comes out clean.

8 Remove skillet from the oven and place on a wire rack. Let cool for 10 minutes. Using a table knife, loosen the edges of the cake. Place a large platter with raised edges over the skillet. Wearing oven mitts, carefully invert cake onto the platter. Remove the skillet. Serve cake warm.

> **TIP** | Use whatever brown sugar you have on hand. In this recipe, light brown sugar will make a lighter-colored caramelized topping (which we prefer), while dark brown sugar will make the topping darker.

Old-Fashioned Gingerbread with Cinnamon Cream

MAKES 10 SERVINGS

Some food experiences become etched in your memory. For Kathy, one of those was a wonderful bite of warm gingerbread in Williamsburg, Virginia. As she was walking the historic streets on a cool, rainy fall day, a bakery was selling slices of freshly baked gingerbread. This recipe is a tasty reminder of that delicious treat.

10-inch (25 cm) cast-iron skillet lined with a 15-inch (38 cm) square of parchment paper
Electric mixer

1½ cups (375 mL) all-purpose flour

2 tsp (10 mL) ground ginger

1½ tsp (7 mL) ground cinnamon

1 tsp (5 mL) baking soda

½ tsp (2 mL) salt

¼ tsp (1 mL) ground cloves

⅔ cup (150 mL) packed dark brown sugar

⅔ cup (150 mL) light (fancy) molasses

⅔ cup (150 mL) boiling water

¼ cup (60 mL) unsalted butter, softened and thinly sliced

1 large egg, at room temperature

CINNAMON CREAM

1 cup (250 mL) heavy or whipping (35%) cream

2 tbsp (30 mL) confectioners' (icing) sugar

½ tsp (2 mL) vanilla extract

¼ tsp (1 mL) ground cinnamon

1 Preheat the oven to 350°F (180°C).

2 In a medium bowl, whisk together flour, ginger, cinnamon, baking soda, salt and cloves. Set aside.

3 In a large bowl, whisk together brown sugar, molasses, boiling water and butter, until butter melts. Let cool for 15 minutes, whisking occasionally.

4 Add egg to molasses mixture; whisk to combine. Add flour mixture; whisk until smooth. Pour into the prepared skillet.

5 Bake in the preheated oven for 35 to 40 minutes or until a tester inserted in the center comes out clean.

6 Remove skillet from the oven and place on a wire rack. Let cool for 15 minutes. Carefully, using the edges of the parchment paper, lift gingerbread out of the skillet. Remove paper and set gingerbread on a serving platter.

7 CINNAMON CREAM Meanwhile, in a small, deep bowl, using an electric mixer at medium-high speed, beat cream until frothy. Gradually beat in confectioners' sugar, vanilla and cinnamon. Continue beating until stiff peaks form. Cut gingerbread into slices and serve each piece with a dollop of cinnamon cream on top.

Caramelized Apple Dutch Baby

MAKES 4 SERVINGS

A Dutch baby is sometimes called a German pancake. It is very fluffy — some describe the texture and appearance as similar to a popover or Yorkshire pudding. The batter is best refrigerated overnight, so plan ahead, but that also makes preparation in the morning a snap.

Blender

10-inch (25 cm) cast-iron skillet

DUTCH BABY BATTER

4 large eggs, at room temperature

⅔ cup (150 mL) milk

½ tsp (2 mL) vanilla extract

⅔ cup (150 mL) all-purpose flour

1 tbsp (15 mL) granulated sugar

⅛ tsp (0.5 mL) salt

Pinch ground nutmeg

1½ tbsp (22 mL) unsalted butter, melted

3 tbsp (45 mL) unsalted butter, cut into 1-tbsp (15 mL) pieces

CARAMELIZED APPLES

¼ cup (60 mL) unsalted butter

2 medium crisp, firm, sweet apples (such as Braeburn, Jazz or Pink Lady), unpeeled and thinly sliced

3 tbsp (45 mL) granulated sugar

½ tsp (2 mL) ground cinnamon

TOPPING

1½ tbsp (22 mL) confectioners' (icing) sugar

1 DUTCH BABY BATTER In a blender, combine eggs, milk and vanilla; blend on high speed until frothy and smooth, about 15 seconds. Add flour, sugar, salt and nutmeg; blend on high speed until smooth. Add melted butter and blend until combined. Transfer to an airtight container and refrigerate for at least 3 hours or preferably overnight.

2 Remove batter from the refrigerator 30 minutes before cooking.

3 Preheat the oven to 400°F (200°C).

4 CARAMELIZED APPLES Meanwhile, melt butter in the skillet over medium heat. Add apples, sugar and cinnamon. Stir to separate the apple slices and coat them evenly with butter and sugar. Reduce heat to medium-low and cook, stirring frequently, for 10 to 15 minutes or until the apples are tender and golden brown. Transfer to a medium bowl, cover and keep warm.

5 DUTCH BABY BATTER Carefully wipe the hot skillet clean and add cut-up 3 tbsp (45 mL) butter. Place skillet in the oven and allow it to heat for 2 to 3 minutes or until butter is melted and bubbling. (Do not allow butter to brown.)

6 Whisk batter and carefully pour into the hot skillet. Bake in the preheated oven for 20 minutes. Reduce the oven temperature to 300°F (150°C). Bake for 5 to 8 minutes more, until the center is golden brown. (If the edges become too brown, cover them with a strip of aluminum foil.) The pancake should be puffed and golden brown.

7 Remove skillet from the oven and place on a wire rack. Top with caramelized apples and sprinkle lightly with confectioners' sugar. Serve immediately.

Cherry Clafouti

MAKES 9 SERVINGS

Several years ago we had the opportunity to work with Northwest Cherry Growers for a promotional event, where we served this showstopping cherry clafouti that we remembered from two decades earlier. While we cannot locate the original recipe, this one tastes like the one we remember. A clafouti is something like a fruit-studded pancake or waffle. This makes a great addition to any brunch or dessert menu.

10-inch (25 cm) cast-iron skillet

Fine-mesh sieve (optional)

4 large eggs, at room temperature

1 cup (250 mL) milk

2 tbsp (30 mL) unsalted butter, melted and cooled slightly

1 tsp (5 mL) vanilla extract

½ cup (125 mL) granulated sugar

½ cup (125 mL) all-purpose flour

2 cups (500 mL) frozen pitted sweet, dark cherries

Confectioners' (icing) sugar (optional)

1 Preheat the oven to 325°F (160°C).

2 In a large bowl, whisk together eggs, milk, melted butter, vanilla and sugar. Sprinkle flour over the mixture and whisk until smooth.

3 Pour batter into the skillet. Sprinkle cherries evenly over the batter. Bake in the preheated oven for 40 to 50 minutes, until the clafouti is puffed and golden.

4 Remove skillet from the oven and place on a wire rack. With a fine-mesh sieve, sift confectioners' sugar lightly overtop (if using). Serve the clafouti immediately.

VARIATION

BLUEBERRY OR RASPBERRY CLAFOUTI
Substitute 1½ cups (375 mL) fresh blueberries or raspberries for the frozen cherries. Proceed with the recipe as directed.

Banana Split Skillet Dump Cake

MAKES 10 SERVINGS

This super-simple, delicious dessert will remind you of a classic banana split, and it takes just minutes to assemble. Dump cakes are best served warm, so this is an ideal after-dinner treat to serve straight from the skillet when family or friends gather at your house.

10-inch (25 cm) cast-iron skillet

6 tbsp (90 mL) unsalted butter, melted and divided

2 bananas, sliced ½ inch (1 cm) thick

1 cup (250 mL) fresh strawberries, sliced

⅓ cup (75 mL) strawberry jam or preserves

1 can (8 oz/250 g) crushed pineapple, with juice

⅓ cup (75 mL) semisweet chocolate chips

1⅔ cups (400 mL) yellow (golden) cake mix (about half of one 15.25 oz/432 g box)

¾ cup (175 mL) half-and-half (10%) cream

Vanilla ice cream (optional)

Maraschino cherries (optional)

1 Preheat the oven to 350°F (180°C).

2 Drizzle 1 tbsp (15 mL) melted butter into the skillet and tilt to coat the bottom. Arrange banana slices evenly in the skillet. Top with strawberries, then dollop jam evenly over everything. Top with pineapple (with juice) and chocolate chips.

3 Sprinkle dry cake mix overtop. Using a fork, break up any large clumps and spread it evenly, taking care not to mound it in the center; do not stir. Drizzle cream and remaining 5 tbsp (75 mL) melted butter slowly over the cake mix to moisten.

4 Bake in the preheated oven for 50 to 55 minutes or until golden brown.

5 Remove skillet from the oven and place on a wire rack. Let cool for 10 minutes. Spoon into individual serving bowls. Top each with a scoop of ice cream and a cherry (if using).

> **TIPS** | In addition to the cherry, let a banana split be your inspiration — top with thawed frozen whipped topping, chocolate or strawberry syrup, chopped peanuts, chopped toasted pecans or sliced fresh strawberries.
>
> Instead of ice cream (or in addition to ice cream if you're feeling extra decadent!), top with thawed frozen whipped topping.

Texas Skillet Cake

MAKES 10 SERVINGS

The upside to this recipe is that it makes just the right number of servings. Traditionally, Texas sheet cake serves a lot of folks; because it's prepared in a sheet pan, it's great for family reunions and parties with lots of people attending. But now you don't need to wait for a crowd to enjoy this cocoa concoction. Mix the batter, bake and enjoy!

10-inch (25 cm) cast-iron skillet

TEXAS CAKE

1 tsp (5 mL) unsalted butter, softened

½ cup (125 mL) water

½ cup (125 mL) unsalted butter, thinly sliced

2 tbsp (30 mL) unsweetened cocoa powder

1 cup (250 mL) all-purpose flour

1 cup (250 mL) granulated sugar

½ tsp (2 mL) baking soda

¼ tsp (1 mL) salt

1 large egg, at room temperature

¼ cup (60 mL) sour cream

1 tsp (5 mL) vanilla extract

CHOCOLATE ICING

3 tbsp (45 mL) milk

2 tbsp (30 mL) unsweetened cocoa powder

¼ cup (60 mL) unsalted butter, thinly sliced

2 cups (500 mL) confectioners' (icing) sugar

3 tbsp (45 mL) chopped toasted pecans (see page 21)

1 Preheat the oven to 350°F (180°C). Grease skillet with softened butter. Set aside.

2 TEXAS CAKE In a small saucepan over medium heat, bring to a boil water, sliced butter and cocoa powder, stirring frequently. Remove from heat.

3 In a large bowl, stir together flour, sugar, baking soda and salt. Stir in egg, sour cream and vanilla. Pour chocolate mixture into the flour mixture and stir until combined and smooth.

4 Pour batter into the prepared skillet. Bake in the preheated oven for 25 to 35 minutes or until a tester inserted in the center comes out clean.

5 Remove skillet from the oven and place on a wire rack.

6 CHOCOLATE ICING Just before the cake is finished baking, combine milk, cocoa powder and butter in a small saucepan over medium heat; bring to a boil, stirring frequently. Remove from heat. Whisk in confectioners' sugar until smooth. When the cake is done and still hot from the oven, pour the icing over the cake. Using the back of a spoon, spread it evenly. Sprinkle pecans evenly over the icing.

ACKNOWLEDGMENTS

Writing each of our cookbooks has been a dream come true for us. We love encouraging people to cook, and our goal is to make cooking easier, tastier and more fun. We are committed to encouraging people to enjoy family dinners at their own table.

Cast iron is part of everyday cooking for us — we use the cookware daily for its excellent performance. We cherish our pans, for we inherited some of them from our moms and grandmas. When we teach, we use several skillets. To make sure we each pack up our own black pans, we had to find a way to mark them. Now all of Kathy's cast-iron pieces have a piece of wire twisted through the hole in the handle so our skillets are easy to tell apart. Some may wonder why we would care so much about specific pans, but we share this story because it reveals the love and deep bonds we feel with all those wonderful cooks in our families who paved the way for us on the culinary path. We are inspired by them and appreciate the skills (and the skillets) they passed on to us. For that reason, we could never fathom losing these family heirlooms.

We wrote this book during the COVID pandemic, a time when we all stayed home, spent more time with our immediate family and learned new skills. Everyone had to adapt to separation from loved ones and friends, grocery shortages, closed restaurants, working from home, homeschooling, illnesses and stress from job loss and the endless impact of the tragic health crisis. Yet, through it all, many of us cooked. We are grateful that, as this manuscript leaves our kitchens and our desks, better times may be in sight. We have all learned that cooking nourishing meals and delicious treats is the sustenance that keeps our families fed in both body and spirit. We have all been reminded that joining together at the table builds sweet memories, provides joy and creates simple pleasures.

A cookbook is truly a group effort. We are grateful to be a part of an incredible team, and we appreciate each and every one of you for your hard work and support. First, we are grateful for our friendship. Sharing both work and friendship with another person is the richest of blessings. A college professor introduced us, and now, decades after we first worked together in that corporate small-appliance test kitchen, we have shared so much of what life offers. From the achievements and sometimes challenges of work to the joys, laughter and support that only lifelong friends can provide, we have continued to be delighted and grateful to be co-authors, business partners and the best of friends.

ROXANNE I would like to thank my mother, who has inspired my love of cooking since I was a little girl. Mom is ninety-one years old and still going strong, still cooking in her cast-iron skillet. She is a true culinary genius who has been sharing her love through food for her entire life. These days her baked treats are an almost daily gift to the other people who live in her condominium complex.

My husband, Bob Bateman, and our daughter, Grace, are my ever-supportive "love team." My world revolves around you. It has been a blessing to prepare meals and bake treats for you all these years. My hope is that those delicious meals and memories convey my love for you. Thank you for always tasting, evaluating and helping with the dishes. I am looking forward to many, many more food adventures and memories around our kitchen table.

KATHY I am ever grateful for the bonds and memories built around our table. For as long as I can remember, meals prepared by my mom and grandmas brought our family together. Today my table is still surrounded with love and traditions. David, Laura and Amanda are my everything. I cannot thank you enough for sharing laughter, time, love, tastes and, of course, those dishes. I love you more than words can express.

We have the very best agents. Sally and Lisa Ekus and the entire team at the Lisa Ekus Group continue to guide and support us. Now, after completing eighteen cookbooks and projects with them, we are immensely grateful for their friendship and for all they do on our behalf.

We are grateful to Bob Dees and Meredith Dees for believing in this cookbook. Your commitment to excellence is inspirational. Rachel Harry, Megan Brush and Parisa Michailidis at Robert Rose Inc. have been so professional; we appreciate each one for their creativity, attention to detail and hard work. We also want to thank Kevin Cockburn for designing this wonderful book, as well as Gillian Watts and Kelly Jones for copyediting, proofreading and indexing it so attentively.

Brian Samuels has made our recipes come alive by capturing the delicious flavors in his beautiful photographs. Thank you, Brian, and Rebecca Arnold Saenz, who assisted on the shoot.

We are always delighted and inspired by the students in our cooking classes and those who we connect with through our blog and social media. Their questions and eagerness to learn make teaching fun and continue to stir us to explore new recipes and techniques. This book is the result of their continued interest in cast-iron cooking and baking.

We appreciate all our colleagues, associates, friends and students who continue to inspire us to learn, share and grow. We are grateful for every one of you and will continue to share our journey on this culinary path at www.pluggedintocooking.com.

INDEX

Library and Archives Canada Cataloguing In Publication

Title: The best cast iron baking book : recipes for breads, pies, biscuits & more /
Roxanne Wyss & Kathy Moore.
Names: Wyss, Roxanne, author. | Moore, Kathy, author.
Description: Includes index.
Identifiers: Canadiana 2021020012X | ISBN 9780778806837 (softcover)
Subjects: LCSH: Skillet cooking. | LCSH: Dutch oven cooking. | LCSH: Cast-iron
cookware. | LCSH: Baking. | LCGFT: Cookbooks.
Classification: LCC TX840.S55 W97 2021 | DDC 641.7/7—dc23